D0555851

Lite and Luscious Cuisine of India

Recipes and tips for healthy and quick meals

Madhu Gadia, M.S., R.D.

Copyright ©1997 by Madhu Gadia

Library of Congress Catalog Card Number 96-92639

Cataloging-in-Publication Data

Gadia, Madhu.

Lite and Luscious Cuisine of India: recipes and tips for healthy and quick meals / Madhu Gadia.

p. cm.

Includes index.

1. Cookery, India. 2. Low-fat diet—recipes. 3. Quick and easy cookery.

4. Diabetes diet—recipes.   I. Title.

TX724.5.I4   1996
641.5954'14—dc20

ISBN 0-9653915-0-7

Edited by: Linda Ross
Typesetting: Shashi K. Gadia
Cover Design: Chad Owen

Printed in the United States of America
Second Printing: 1998

Published by:
Piquant publishing
P.O. Box 784
Ames, IA 50010-0784
(515) 292-7170

Dedicated to
my mom and dad

Acknowledgments

I would like to take this opportunity to thank the people who helped make this book possible:

My mother, Satya Vati Gupta, for teaching me the art and love of cooking.

My father, Vimal Kishore Gupta, for his world of wisdom and love of life.

My husband Shashi for his love and technical support. The computer makes writing much easier these days, but it doesn't always behave the way I want it to. He always knew what to do with it.

My daughter Manisha and son Nitin; they were always eager to try the recipes. Manisha, for doing most of the line art pieces.

My sister Shelly for her encouragement, ideas and proofreading of the recipes in the initial stages and doing some of the line art pieces. She was always eager to help.

My brother-in-law Rajeev Nath for offering to read and edit portions of the book. I sincerely appreciate his taking time out of his busy schedule for my work.

Priya Kothari, my daughter's friend for taking the time out of her summer to help with the line art. She did all the figure drawing.

Dr. Meg Tait, for reviewing the nutrition section.

Margaret Junken, owner of Cook's Emporium, for giving me the opportunity to teach cooking classes. I appreciate her excitement and love for cooking. I enjoy browsing in her store and appreciate her lending me the dishes and accessories for the pictures.

Shellie Robson of Robson and Associates Publishing Services for her expert advice, encouragement and availability.

Linda Ross for her time and expertise in editing the book.

Chad Owen for designing the cover.

Iacovas Zachariades for scanning and touching up the pictures. His enthusiasm and flexibility was very helpful.

Thanks to all the people who took my cooking classes. Their enthusiasm to learn new cuisine and taste for Indian food gave me a head start.

My clients who come to decipher nutrition information and take better care of their bodies. They make my job fun and exciting. I learn so much from them.

Contents

Introduction

Food has a language of its own. "What's for dinner?" is probably the most-common phrase spoken in every language of the world. Something about the aroma of cooking is very soothing to the body and soul. Nothing brings a family together like a home cooked meal. As a child growing up in India, I remember becoming hungry as the smell of food filled the air. The family would sit down to a meal together and exchange the day's events. Suddenly I felt nourished with both food and love. I remember going on the train to my grandmother's house. At the train station I always looked for the same vendor who was famous for his *samosas* (potato-stuffed pastry). His *samosas* were like no one else's we ever ate. These memories are very personal and very close to my heart. A taste or smell of food can take me down memory lane without ever leaving my house.

When I came to America, I wondered if I would be able to get my favorite and familiar foods. My fears were ill-founded. I easily found most of the needed ingredients. If something was not available locally, I could mail order it from Indian grocery stores in large cities. Over the years the availability of Indian spices and other special ingredients has increased tremendously as more local grocery stores and specialty stores cater to different ethnic populations.

Indian cuisine is becoming increasingly popular in America. Two years ago, I learned that some people in my small city Ames, Iowa, were interested in learning Indian cooking. I decided to offer a class. As I started to prepare for the class, I realized that I did not have any written recipes. I learned to cook from my mother and she from her mother. The art of cooking in India is passed on in this way from generation to generation. If you asked an Indian friend how to prepare something, he or she would verbally tell you with approximate measures. Well, that would not work in a class setting. So I started writing my own recipes.

Indian cooking varies from region to region with wheat as the main staple in the north and northwest and rice as the main staple in the south and southeast. Spices are the key to Indian cuisine and give the foods their delightful flavors. Each region has specific spices and blends that give each food its unique taste. I grew up in a cosmopolitan university town in north India. Therefore, I had the pleasure of eating foods from all over India. My mother enjoyed learning to cook dishes from different regions of India and I was fortunate to learn from her. In the seventies and onward the mobility of people has increased. As people leave home and experience the new lands they also experience new flavors and cuisines. In India now you can find *idli-dosa* (south Indian specialty) in Delhi and *puri-chole* (north Indian specialty) in Madras. Not only has the food within India become versatile but international cuisines are becoming very popular. As we taste a variety of food our tastebuds have gone international. In this book you will find recipes from various regions of India.

A nutritional look at Indian food

As a registered dietitian I am always concerned about the nutrient content of foods. The USDA's (United States Department of Agriculture) "The Dietary Guidelines for Americans" recommends a diet high in carbohydrate and fiber and low in fat and saturated fat. Indian meals, with plenty of vegetables, beans and pulses, are generally high in carbohydrate and fiber. The fat content of some Indian dishes may be high but over the years I have successfully reduced the amount of fat used in preparing many traditional Indian dishes. Reducing the fat content can mean using less fat, or it may require variation in spices or cooking techniques. I have experimented and developed the recipes to reduce the fat content while maintaining the traditional flavor and taste.

Vegetarian meals are becoming more acceptable and popular in the Western World. As part of a diet low in saturated fat and cholesterol, reducing the intake of meat, poultry and fish is recommended. Vegetarian meals are part of the daily diet in India. A significant percentage of Indians are lactovegetarians—vegetarians who include dairy products in their diets. Even nonvegetarians in India do not eat meat at every meal or every day, and all auspicious occasions exclude meat due to religious beliefs. Indians have combined beans, vegetables, grains and yogurt in a meal for centuries. Combining of these foods was later classified as a way of getting "complete protein". Indian vegetarian meals are delicious, exciting and nutritious.

A nutritional analysis for each recipe is provided for major nutrients like calories, grams of fat, saturated fat, cholesterol, carbohydrate, dietary fiber, protein and sodium. Exchange information based on the Exchange List for Meal Planning is also provided for each recipe. This information is particularly helpful for people with special dietary needs like diabetes, heart disease and hypertension.

No time to cook

With the busy lifestyle of the nineties who has enough time to cook elaborate meals that take hours to prepare? As a working mother, I prepare most of the meals for my family in less than one hour. Over the years, I have learned many time-saving techniques that help in getting that favorite meal on the table with minimum time. The majority of Indian cooking is done on the stove top. With modern appliances, a stove with four burners and a little preparation, a delicious, authentic Indian meal can be prepared quickly and efficiently.

The recipes offered in this book have been carefully tested for accuracy. Several of the recipes were offered in the cooking class and retested by the students. My family, friends and students have enjoyed serving as the official taste testers.

The purpose of this book is to provide recipes for healthy, low fat, quick, authentic Indian meals that are both delicious and nutritious. For those looking for a little spice in their life, whether on a low-cholesterol diet, follow a diabetic meal plan, vegetarian diet, cutting down on fat intake or simply wanting great tasting Indian food, this book will offer a variety of dishes to please their taste buds.

India

Healthy weight

Healthy body weight? What is it? Over the years what is healthy and acceptable seems to have changed. This is the era of weight-conscious people. We always seem to be reminded of what we can do to lose weight. Genetics aside, what we eat and how we live contribute to where the numbers fall on the bathroom scale.

All the research indicates that excess weight is linked to many serious illnesses including heart disease, high blood pressure, diabetes and cancer. Yet as the years go by people are getting heavier. Americans on the average weigh ten pounds more than their counterparts did a decade ago. Why is it so difficult to lose weight and keep it off? Every day there are new diets in magazines, on television or in new books. It seems there is a new diet born every minute. In my practice, as I take food intake and weight history, I see the frustration of people who have tried every diet and lost countless pounds only to regain them. Part of the problem is we all want a quick fix. People fall prey to any quick-fix scheme that promises weight loss with minimum effort. What I have learned from my clients and personal life experiences is that nothing comes from nothing and every change takes time and effort.

The main problem is the word *diet*. Actually the word *diet* means your total daily food intake. Now the word diet has become associated with restricted food intake that is designed to promote weight loss. Unfortunately it has even found its way into the children's vocabulary. Children should not be subjected to weight loss diets (unless medically warranted). Children should be provided with variety of foods, love and encouraged to be active and healthy. Weight loss diets often cause obsession with food and therefore make it more difficult to maintain a healthy natural weight.

No more diet

Weight loss experts say that part of the problem is our approach. Going on a diet is the wrong method. Diet is typically thought of as a temporary change lasting just long enough to lose the excess weight and then returning to old habits. The word diet has negative connotations and many of my clients say that just the mention of diet makes them crazy; yet, they come for another diet. Dieting is a vicious circle. When people go on a diet they get hungry and denial and deprivation leads to overeating or *bingeing*. Then comes guilt, "I can not do this, I can not trust myself" and they start all over—another diet, (See Diet-Binge cycle below.) Unfortunately, this cycle sets in sooner or later and sabotages most weight loss efforts.

However, people don't have to deny themselves all the foods they like in order to lose weight, and we know that anything that is forbidden has special power and attraction.

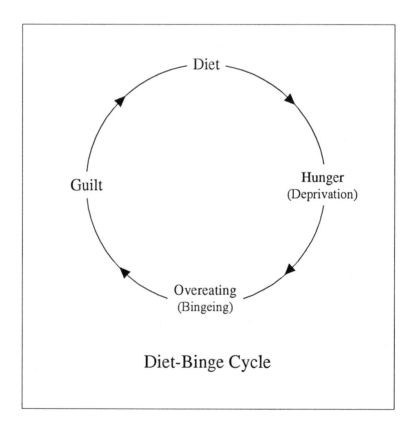

Diet

Guilt

Hunger
(Deprivation)

Overeating
(Bingeing)

Diet-Binge Cycle

What can one do?

So if one is not supposed to go on a diet, what is one supposed to do? Most people gain weight gradually, about 2–5 pounds per year. They are surprised when ten years later they are 20–50 pounds over their young adult weight. The basic fact of maintaining weight is to balance "calories in" and "calories out." If over the years a person has gradually reduced activity (calories out) and increased intake (calories in), some weight gain is inevitable. However, if we used our hunger as a barometer of when to eat, then the balance would be maintained. As children, we were in touch with our hunger; if we were full we stopped eating. Weight gain occurs when we do some nonhunger eating.

I often hear from my clients that they are always hungry or starved—that their appetite is insatiable. My first step is to help them see the difference between physical and psychological hunger. *Physical hunger* is real, it comes from the stomach and food satisfies it. *Psychological*

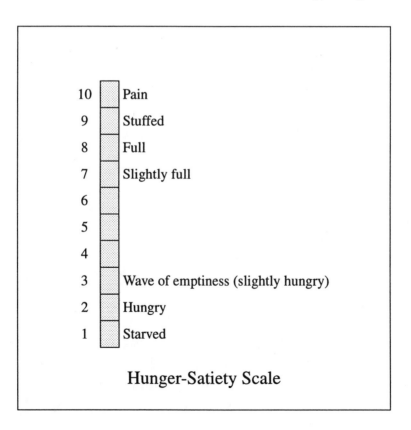

10	Pain
9	Stuffed
8	Full
7	Slightly full
6	
5	
4	
3	Wave of emptiness (slightly hungry)
2	Hungry
1	Starved

Hunger-Satiety Scale

hunger, the desire for food, is a learned response and is impossible to satisfy with food. Once the person knows the difference between the two hungers it is easier to deal with food-related issues. Here is a scale to help you decide where you fall. (See Hunger-Satiety Scale on page 7.) Think of hunger on a scale from 1 to 10. One is empty or starved and 10 is overstuffed or in pain. Ask yourself where are you right now on the scale of 1 to 10. Then sit down and take a few deep breaths to relax. Relax from head to toe and when you are completely relaxed, put your hands on your stomach and ask your stomach where it is from 1 to 10. Is it the same or different than what you thought you were before you relaxed and put your hands on your stomach? People often feel hungry when they are not. Some of the reasons that can cause them to eat are boredom, anger, anxiety, stress, fatigue, sight or smell of food and habit. These psychological hungers are not felt in the stomach. So before each meal and snack, relax and ask yourself if you are "stomach hungry," how hungry are you, and what it will take to satisfy that hunger. If your stomach is not hungry ask yourself what are you feeling (bored, tired, etc.) and then resolve that feeling instead. If you do not know what you are feeling but know that your stomach is not hungry, try something to take care of yourself like taking a bath, listening to music or going for a walk. Ask yourself later what you were feeling. After all, if you are not hungry, food won't really take care of you or help to solve the problem.

With practice and time you can distinguish between the two hungers. Soon that hunger will become your guide to freedom and you will gradually change your eating habits. Remember, hunger is the spice that makes food taste great.

Low fat foods for healthy weight

Eating low fat foods can lead to long-term benefits. Eating lower fat foods on a regular basis with occasional higher fat foods adds that variety and avoids deprivation.

The portions are very important. People feel they can eat all they want as long as the food is fat free or low fat. That is very misleading. Remember, a person can eat all the right foods but if he or she eats more than what the body needs (beyond full on the hunger scale), weight gain will occur. The body knows only one way to store an excess intake of food (calories) and that is as fat.

Some basic tips for a healthy lifestyle

Contrary to popular belief *eating healthy* doesn't have to be boring or take a long time to prepare. Nor does it take special foods. Health and taste are not mutually exclusive. With a little creativity and careful selection, healthy dining can be enjoyed by the whole family and taste divine. Here are some tips to help you begin eating healthy for life.

- To get started, keep a food diary for at least a week. Remember to write down all the meals and snacks. Anything that goes in your mouth goes in the diary. This will help you to see how much, how often, where and when you eat. See Food Record on page 10.

- Pay attention to the hunger scale. See how often you ate when you were not hungry or ate beyond full. How did you feel? What were you feeling that might have contributed to this eating? The more detailed your records are, the more you will learn about your eating habits. Review the diary and you may be surprised at some of the eating habits that you have developed over the years without realizing it. This diary can be your road map to change.

- Exercise is an important integral part of healthy lifestyle. Exercise can vary from day to day. Try to add some physical activity at least three times a week. Start gradually and build up tolerance. I tell my clients to start increasing activity from where they are comfortable, one block, two blocks, 5 minutes or 20 minutes, and increase gradually at their own pace. Do what you like rather than what you should. Just do something.

- Eat three meals per day. Skipping meals typically sabotages weight loss efforts. For example, if I skip lunch I find myself snacking at 3:00 and then eating more at dinner and maybe a late night snack, based on the rationale that I skipped lunch. If for any reason you have to skip a meal and end up with a snack, call it a meal even if it consists of snack foods.

- Getting on the bathroom scale once a day is a terrible way to start a day. Many weight loss experts advise throwing out the scale altogether. Weight loss—at least the kind that lasts—is the kind that occurs with

Food Record

Time	Food intake	Amount	Hunger 1 2 3 4 5 6 7 8 9 10	Place*	Feelings
8:20	Whole wheat toast	2	2------------7	DR	Rushed
	Margarine	1 tsp			
	Tea with milk	1 cup			
	Sugar	2 tsp			

* DR–dinning room, LR–living room, BR–bed room, KI–kitchen, OF–office, RS–restaurant, OT–other, where?

change in eating and exercise habits. The weight loss will happen so slowly that weighing yourself more than once a week could easily sabotage your efforts. I tell my clients that your weight is not in your control but your eating habits are. Pay attention to what and why you eat and your weight will take care of itself. Besides, your clothes will tell you how you are progressing.

- Be flexible about a time limit for weight loss. Make changes gradually and make them last. Losing one pound per week is considered an excellent weight loss.

- Avoid fad diets. A *fad diet* is one that promises quick weight loss with minimum or no effort. Avoid any diet that skips a whole food group. It is nutritionally unbalanced and can lead to health risks. Avoid deprivation.

- Choose foods you like. For example, if you skip your favorite cookie, what happens. You will probably eat twice that number of calories in other foods and then might eat that cookie anyway. Work in foods you like and learn to adjust for them.

- Eat in a positive and deliberate manner. Avoid chaotic eating. Get a plate, take a piece of cake, sit down and enjoy every bite. Then go on your merry way.

- Monitor portion sizes. Your eyes tend to be bigger than your stomach.

- Pay attention to the hunger scale. If you are full, stop eating. It is terrible to waste food but if you eat when you are full, just so you don't have to throw it away, it is still wasted. *Waste versus Waist.*

- Avoid grazing through the kitchen. If you are hungry, take a minute to decide what are you hungry for, and then eat that.

- Avoid eating when you are not hungry. If you are tired, rest for 10 minutes; if you are bored do something different or call a friend. Make a list of things you like to do and have to do. The list can help you when you can not think of what to do.

- Eating foods lower in fat can help with the process of gradual change. Fat is an acquired taste. As you slowly reduce the fat intake in your diet, your palate and desire for high fat foods decreases.

- Keep the pantry and refrigerator stocked with whole grains, fruits and vegetables.

- Limit eating out. When eating out, it is too easy to eat too much, especially foods high in fat.
- Plan your meals at home before meal times. Someone once said, "If you don't plan you plan to fail."
- If you feel you don't have time to cook, use the tips given in the section of Time-savings tips to prepare meals on those rushed days.

Cholesterol and fat

Low fat and *cholesterol free* are the words for nineties. Low fat, fat free and cholesterol free products are springing up everywhere. Limiting fat and cholesterol is an important step you can take toward better health. The American Heart Association, American Institute for Cancer Research and the American Diabetes Association recommend a meal plan low in fat and cholesterol for better health and disease prevention. High fat diets are linked to heart disease, certain types of cancer, diabetes mellitus and weight gain. By understanding where cholesterol and fat comes from in your diet, it is easier to follow the recommendations set forth.

High blood cholesterol is one of the major risk factors for coronary heart disease. Anyone can develop high blood cholesterol. There are no warning symptoms or signs. If your blood cholesterol is high, you need to find out how high it is and learn what you can do to lower it. Compare your numbers with the numbers in the table Cholesterol Levels, given below. The preferred way to lower your cholesterol is to modify your lifestyle.

	Desirable	Borderline High Risk	High Risk
Cholesterol	less than 200 mg/dl	200–239 mg/dl	240 mg/dl and greater
HDL-Cholesterol	35 mg/dl or greater		less than 35 mg/dl
LDL-Cholesterol	less than 130 mg/dl	130–159 mg/dl	160 mg/dl and greater

Cholesterol Levels

Cholesterol

Cholesterol is essential to life. Every cell in our body requires cholesterol in its membranes. Cholesterol is also important for many functions of the body. The liver is capable of making all the cholesterol that is needed. If no cholesterol is eaten, the body would produce the cholesterol needed. Cholesterol is a member of the lipid family. The more-common name for lipid is fat. Cholesterol is not synonymous with fat. Even though it is usually associated with fat, it is a separate lipid. Many foods also provide cholesterol. Cholesterol only comes from foods of animal origin such as meat, poultry, seafood and dairy products. *Food can be cholesterol-free but still high in total fat.*

Excess cholesterol, along with other substances, is deposited in the inside walls of the arteries, causing plaque buildup. Atherosclerosis (hardening of the arteries) occurs when plaque builds up in the walls of the arteries that supply blood to the heart. These deposits narrow the arteries and can slow or block the flow of blood.

Knowing your high density lipoprotein (HDL) and low density lipoprotein (LDL) is also beneficial in determining your risk factor for heart disease. HDL-cholesterol is referred to as the "good cholesterol" as it helps prevent accumulation of cholesterol in the walls of the arteries. You want your HDL-cholesterol to be high. LDL-cholesterol is referred to as the "bad cholesterol" as it carries most of the cholesterol and causes plaque buildup. You want your LDL-cholesterol to be low. Ask your physician for a complete workup of your lipid levels. Know your numbers and compare them to desirable levels.

There are several factors that affect your cholesterol levels:

1. Eating habits
2. Weight
3. Physical activity or exercise
4. Genetic factors
5. Age
6. Stress

The important thing to know is that you can do something about many of these risk factors. By changing eating and exercise habits, reducing weight if needed and learning stress management, many people are able to lower their blood cholesterol levels.

An eating plan to lower high blood cholesterol

The primary treatment for high blood cholesterol is an eating plan *low in total fat*, especially saturated fat and cholesterol.

Saturated fats

Saturated fats raise cholesterol levels more than anything else in your diet. Saturated fat are mostly found in animal products and in some plant products. Saturated fats are solid at room temperature. Animal sources of saturated fats are egg yolks, meat, poultry, fish and dairy products. Plant sources include coconut, coconut oil, palm oil, palm kernel oil and cocoa butter. Please note: *A food may be cholesterol free but still be high in saturated fat.*

Unsaturated fats

Unsaturated fats include polyunsaturated and monounsaturated fats. Unsaturated fats are liquid at room temperature. Studies indicate that both of these fats help lower the blood cholesterol level. Good sources of polyunsaturated fats are safflower, sunflower, corn and soybean oil. The major sources of monounsaturated fats are olive, peanut and canola oil.

Hydrogenated fats

Hydrogenated fats are liquid oils that are converted to solid or semisolid form. Shortening and margarine are example of hydrogenated fats. Hydrogenated fats contain more saturated fats than liquid oils. Use these fats sparingly. Margarine contains partially hydrogenated oils, so choose margarine made with "liquid" vegetable oil as the first ingredient.

The cholesterol intake should be limited to less than 300 mg per day. The total fat should be limited to less than 30 percent of the calories and saturated fat to less than 10 percent of the calories. The daily fat budget depends on the number of calories consumed in the day.

Calculate your daily calorie needs

To determine your caloric needs, take your present weight and multiply by your activity level.

- Weight × 13 for a sedentary lifestyle (no aerobic exercise on regular basis)
- Weight × 15 for a moderately active lifestyle (aerobic exercise for 20–30 minutes, 2–3 times per week)
- Weight × 17 for an active lifestyle (aerobic exercise 4–5 times per week)
- Weight × 20 for a very active lifestyle (very physical job plus aerobic exercise 6–7 times per week)

Calories come from the carbohydrate, protein and fat in our diet. There are 4 calories per gram in carbohydrates and proteins and 9 calories per gram in fats. Fat therefore, is more than twice as dense in calories.

Calculate your daily fat "budget"

Once you have determined your caloric needs, then you can determine your daily fat limits, using the following formula or the chart. Remember that this should be your maximum fat intake per day. On most days you should keep your fat intake at or below this level.

Formula

By using this formula you can calculate the grams of fat based on your daily caloric intake. It also allows you to individualize the percent fat, if desired. For example you can calculate 25 percent fat instead of 30.

Calories × 30/100 = calories from fat

Calories from fat ÷ 9 = grams of fat

For example: 1500 calories × 30/100 = 450 calories from fat

450 ÷ 9 = 50 grams of fat

Chart

Use the table given on the next page to estimate your daily fat and saturated fat limits.

Daily calories	Maximum fat (30% of calories)	Maximum saturated fat (10% of calories)
1200	40 grams	13 grams
1500	50 grams	17 grams
1800	60 grams	20 grams
2000	67 grams	22 grams
2500	83 grams	28 grams

Fat and cholesterol in Indian meals

Typical Indian meals use liberal amounts of vegetables and grains. Since about one third of the Indians are vegetarians, vegetarian meals are predominant in Indian diets. Meat and eggs are used in moderation by nonvegetarians. Hindus typically avoid beef and Muslims avoid pork. Overall, the diet is high in complex carbohydrates and fiber.

Generally, the concern is the liberal use of oil and ghee (clarified butter) in cooking. The food is often roasted or sauteed (bhuna) in liberal amounts of ghee/oil or deep-fat fried. Therefore, the total fat intake of that meal may be high. Ghee is often used in cooking, which increases the saturated fat intake. In several dishes of south Indian origin, coconut is used, which is also high in saturated fat. For general guide to fat and cholesterol in Indian foods, see the table General Guide to Fat and Cholesterol on page 18.

I have modified the traditional Indian recipes to reduce the fat content. In some recipes ghee or coconut is used but only in small quantities. Whenever possible, a liquid vegetable oil is used. Use your favorite liquid oil for cooking. It is well known that fat adds flavor to the recipes. But the amount of fat needed can be reduced without altering the traditional taste and flavor. If any one method was to be called the Indian way of cooking, it would be roasting in a pan using oil. This process is called "bhun-na." The spices are roasted in oil to make a masala (spice mixture), and then the meat or vegetables are roasted with masala to bring out the flavor of the spices as well as the other ingredients. This process also gives the gravy or curry its unique taste. The same *bhuna* taste can achieved by altering the process slightly.

General Guide to Fat and Cholesterol

Food	Serving size	Fat (gm)	Sat. fat (gm)	Chol (mg)
Beverages				
Nonfat beverages like coffee, tea, juices, mineral water, soft drinks	1 cup	0	0	0
Breads and starches				
Rice, pasta	½ cup	0	0	0
Bread, chapati (6 inch diameter)	1	< 1	0	0
Fruits and vegetables				
All fruits and vegetables except olives and avocados	½–1 cup	0	0	0
Dairy products				
Whole milk	1 cup	8	5	33
Low fat milk, yogurt	1 cup	5	3	18
Skim milk, non fat yogurt	1 cup	< 1	< 1	4
Cheese like cheddar, American	1 oz	9	6	30
Cheese, low fat like part skim mozzarella	1 oz	6	4	22
Paneer	¼ cup	8	5	33
Meat and substitutes, cooked				
Chicken, no skin	3 oz	6	2	75
Lean beef, chuck	3 oz	10	4	80
Lean pork, loin	3 oz	12	4	75
Lean lamb, leg	3 oz	7	2	75
Fish, white	3 oz	1	0	40
Shellfish like shrimp	3 oz	1	< 1	150
Egg	1	5	2	274
Beans	½ cup	0	0	0
Fats and oils				
Margarine	1 tsp	5	1	0
Butter	1 tsp	5	3	11
Cream, whipping light	1 tbsp	5	3	17
Half-and-half	2 tbsp	5	2	12
Ghee	1 tsp	5	3	10
Vegetable oil	1 tsp	5	< 1	0
Coconut, fresh	1 oz	8	7	0
Coconut, desiccated	1 oz	18	16	0
Coconut milk	¼ cup	14	12	0
Coconut oil	1 tsp	5	4	0
Nuts like peanuts	1 oz	14	2	0

Fat is an acquired taste. I always tell my clients that by gradually cutting down on fat intake, your pallet adjusts and actually enjoys the real taste of food. Low fat meals or foods feel much better to our system and we feel lighter and more energetic. High fat foods are heavy in the stomach and we feel lethargic after eating them. One example of an acquired taste is the fact that most people used whole milk not too long ago and now many have switched to low fat or skim milk. They now find drinking whole milk too rich and not as palatable as they once did.

It is specially easy to eat low fat foods if they taste good. Every effort is used to preserve the traditional flavor and taste. Most dishes are low fat with only the minimum amount of fat used to bring out the flavor and taste. Low fat cooking is a good way to cut down on fat intake without compromising taste. A few fried foods and desserts are included to serve on special occasions.

Moderation and variety is the key to good health. I have served low fat meals to my unsuspecting family and guests for years; the way they seemed to enjoy the food I would say they did not miss a thing. You will find these dishes easy to fit into most meal plans.

Here are some easy tips to reduce fat and cholesterol intake:

- Use more fruits and vegetables. Five servings of fruits and vegetables per day is recommended.
- Use more foods (high fiber) like whole grains, dried beans, peas and lentils.
- Choose some meatless meals each week by using beans or lentils for a complete meal.
- Use less oil in sauteing or roasting spices.
- Avoid deep-fried foods or limit how often you eat them.
- Use condiments and spices to add flavor to recipes.
- Choose skim milk or 1% milk and its products.
- Choose nonfat yogurt and buttermilk.
- Avoid whole milk, cream, sour cream and half-and-half. Substitute evaporated skim milk or nonfat yogurt where possible.

- Limit the quantity of meat, poultry and seafood to 6 ounces (cooked weight) per day.
- Choose poultry and fish more often than red meat.
- Remove the skin from chicken before cooking.
- Choose only lean meats and trim all visible fat before cooking. Look for meat that has little or no marbling of fat. Choose meats that have 3 grams or less fat per ounce.
- Avoid high fat meats like spareribs, frankfurters, sausage and regular cold cuts.
- Use 2 egg whites versus a whole egg in recipes.
- Limit the use of ghee and butter.
- Limit the use of coconut, coconut milk and coconut oil.
- Choose liquid oils like safflower, sunflower, corn, soybean, olive or canola oil for most of your cooking.
- Choose a margarine that contains twice as much polyunsaturated as saturated fat.
- Use salad dressings sparingly. Use low fat or fat free dressings whenever possible.
- Nuts and seeds contain unsaturated fats, but in general are very high in fat. Use sparingly.
- Monitor the size of your portions. You can occasionally eat somethings high in fat if consumed in small portions. Also you can eat too much of the right food. (Excess calories can only be stored as fat in your body.)
- Keep your fat budget in mind. If you go over your fat budget one day, balance it the next day.
- Be aware of hidden fats. Hidden fats are in desserts, pastries, dairy products, prepared dishes and fried foods.
- Read food labels. Food labels can give you information on total fat, cholesterol and saturated fat. (Rule of thumb: If something has 3 grams of fat and 100 calories, it has approximately 30% fat).
- A secret to serving low fat meals: Do not tell your family or guests you have used a low fat recipe or cut down the fat in the dish until after they have eaten and enjoyed it.

Exchanges for meal planning

Weight loss diets and exchanges

Many weight loss programs use the exchange lists for meal planning. This allows the individuals more variety and flexibility to plan meals. The exchanges provided for each recipe in this book can be easily calculated for meal plans.

A word about diabetes

The results of a ten-year study, the Diabetes Control and Complications Trial (DCCT), clearly demonstrated that blood glucose control effectively delays the onset and slows the progression of long-term complications of type I diabetes: retinopathy, nephropathy, neuropathy and others.

Since the complications of diabetes are similar in both type I and type II diabetes, it is assumed that keeping blood glucose control as near to normal as possible is just as important for persons with type II diabetes as for those with type I diabetes. Any effort to control blood sugars helps reduce long-term complications.

Nutrition therapy is integral to total diabetes care and management. Nutrition and meal planning principles are among the most-challenging aspects of diabetes care. The DCCT emphasized the importance of individualized meal plans in achieving and maintaining desired blood glucose levels. A registered dietitian (RD) can individualize the meal plan based on the present nutritional status, lifestyle and medications needed to control diabetes.

The 1994 nutrition recommendations from the American Diabetes Association recommend that the percentage of calories from carbohydrate and fat should be individualized based on assessment and treatment goals. The saturated fat should be limited to 10 percent or less of the total calories and the dietary cholesterol should be limited to 300 mg or less per day. The guidelines for protein is 10–20 percent of the total calories.

The management of diabetes requires balancing of food, activity and medication (insulin and/or oral hypoglycemic agents), if needed. When one eats, the blood glucose (sugar) levels rise. The first step in diabetes meal planning is making healthy food choices as it can affect the blood glucose control. People with diabetes do not need special foods. In fact, the diabetic meal plan is good for the whole family.

Some basic suggestions for management of diabetes

- Eat meals and snack at regular times every day.
- Avoid skipping meals. Skipping meals or snack can cause large swings in blood glucose levels.
- Eat about the same amount of food at the same time each day.
- Eat a wide variety of foods every day.
- Choose foods high in fiber like fruits, vegetables, whole grains and beans. High fiber foods are filling and may lower blood and blood fat levels.
- Eat less added fat, sugar and salt.
- If one needs to lose weight, reduce portion sizes.
- Physical activity and exercise can help improve blood glucose control. Exercise contributes to overall health status of all persons with diabetes.
- Self blood glucose monitoring helps provide important information toward blood glucose control. Consult a physician if needed.

Exchange lists for meal planning

Exchange lists for meal planning, developed by the American Diabetes Association and the American Dietetic Association, is one of the tools often used for planning a diet to control diabetes. There are six exchanges or food groups. Foods with similar calories, carbohydrate, protein and fat are grouped together in each exchange list.

The six food groups or exchange lists and the nutrient content in one serving are given in Exchange Lists below.

Food groups/ Lists	Carbohydrate (gm)	Protein (gm)	Fat (gm)	Calories
Starches	15	3	0–1	80
Fruits	15	0	0	60
Milk				
Skim	12	8	0–3	90
Low fat	12	8	5	120
Whole	12	8	8	150
Vegetables	5	2	0	25
Meat and meat substitutes				
Lean	0	7	0–3	35–55
Medium high	0	7	5	75
High fat	0	7	8	100
Fats	0	0	5	45

Exchange Lists

A meal pattern based on the exchange lists enables an individual to exchange or trade one food for another in the same group. This helps to include a wide variety of foods in the daily meals without affecting blood sugars significantly and at the same time to keep the calories and nutrient values consistent.

Each recipe in this book has the exchanges listed. Every effort has been made to calculate the exchanges as would best fit within the calories, carbohydrate, protein and fat. Please remember that the nutrient value for each exchange list are averages and are not always the exact values for a specific food within the exchange list.

Constant carbohydrate diet

Some people find that simply counting carbohydrates provides a more-flexible approach than the exchange groups. This method basically monitors the carbohydrate intake. The principle of the constant carbohydrate diet is that all carbohydrates have a similar affect on blood sugar. In this approach the starches, fruits and milk can be interchanged as they have approximately 15 grams of carbohydrates per exchange or serving. The meal plan provides a suggested pattern of intake such as 45 grams of carbohydrate at breakfast, 60 grams at lunch, 75 grams for dinner and 20 grams for a snack. In this approach the insulin can be adjusted based on the carbohydrate intake of the meal.

The carbohydrate content of each recipe is given. Indian meals are typically high in carbohydrates. They can be easily worked into a constant carbohydrate diet. Adjust the insulin intake, if needed.

Exchange lists

The following pages list foods for each of the exchange groups and their nutritional content, as well as free and combination foods. Free foods have less than 20 calories per serving. The combination foods are those that represent more than one exchange group. The exchange lists also includes foods specific to Indian meals. Each food is listed with its serving size, which is usually measured after cooking.

Starches

One serving has 80 calories,
15 grams carbohydrate,
3 grams protein and
less than 1 gram fat.

Bread, dinner roll	1 slice (1 oz)
Bun, hamburger or hot dog, English muffin, bagel	½ (1 oz)
Cereal flakes, unsweetened	¾ cup
Cereal, cooked	½ cup
Crackers, low fat	6–8 (1 oz)
Flour, wheat, white, corn	3 tbsp
Pasta, noodles	½ cup
Pita, naan	½ (1 oz)
Popcorn, air popped	3 cups
Rice, cooked	⅓ cup
Tortilla, phulka, roti, chapati (6–7 inch diameter)	1

Starchy vegetables

Corn, green peas, cooked	½ cup
Corn on the cob, 6 inch long	1
Mixed vegetables with corn, peas or pasta	1 cup
Potatoes, cooked	½ cup
Sweet potatoes, yams, plantain	½ cup
Squash, pumpkin category	1 cup

Beans (Count as one starch and one lean meat exchange.)

Dried bean, peas, lentils or dal, cooked	½ cup

Fruits

One serving has 60 calories,
15 grams carbohydrate,
0 grams protein and
0 grams fat.

Apple, banana, pear,	1 small (4 oz)
Orange, peach, nectarine, kiwi	1 medium
Cantaloupe, honeydew	1 cup cubes
Grapefruit, large	½
Grapes	17 (3 oz)
Mango, small	½ fruit or ½ cup
Papaya	1 cup cubes
Plums	2
Watermelon	1¼ cup cubes
Dates, prunes	3
Raisins	2 tbsp

Canned fruits packed in its own juice or in extra light syrup

Pineapple, pears, peaches, cherries, apricots, fruit cocktail	½ cup

Fruit juice

Apple, grapefruit, orange, pineapple	½ cup
Prune, cranberry, grape juice	⅓ cup

Milk

One serving has 90 calories,
12 grams carbohydrate,
8 grams protein and
1–3 grams fat.

Skim milk, ½%, 1%	1 cup
Evaporated skim milk	½ cup
Nonfat, low fat buttermilk	1 cup
Nonfat dry milk powder	⅓ cup
Plain nonfat yogurt	1 cup
Light, sugar free yogurt	1 cup

Lowfat and whole milk

Lowfat milk, 2% (5 grams fat)	1 cup
Lowfat yogurt, plain (5 grams fat)	1 cup
Whole milk (8 grams fat)	1 cup

Vegetables

One serving has 25 calories,
5 grams carbohydrates,
2 grams protein and
0 grams fat.

Vegetables that contain small amounts of carbohydrate and calories are on this list. Starchy vegetables are included in the starch list. If you eat 1 or 2 servings of vegetables from this list at a meal, you do not have to count the calories or the carbohydrates because they contain only small amounts of these nutrients. (Raw vegetables, when cooked, decrease in volume.)

One vegetable exchange is as follows:

- ½ cup of cooked vegetables or vegetable juice
- 1 cup of raw vegetables

Beans: green, wax, Italian, Indian
Broccoli
Cabbage
Carrots
Cauliflower
Cucumber
Eggplant
Gourds: bitter, bottle, ridge
Greens: mustard, collard, turnip, spinach
Mushrooms
Okra
Onions
Pea pods
Peppers, all varieties
Radishes
Salad greens: lettuce, romaine, escarole
Tomatoes
Tomato/vegetable juice
Turnips
Zucchini

Meat and meat substitutes

Very lean and lean meat and substitutes
One serving has 35–55 calories,
0 grams carbohydrates,
7 grams protein and
0–3 grams fat.

Beef, lean, less than 10% fat such as sirloin, chuck, round, rib eye, flank steak, tenderloin, ground round	1 oz
Pork, lean, less than 10% fat such as ham, Canadian bacon, tenderloin, center chops, leg roast	1 oz
Poultry: chicken, turkey (no skin)	1 oz
Fish, any fresh or frozen	1 oz
Shellfish: clams, crab, lobster, scallops, shrimp	2 oz
Pheasant, duck, goose (no skin)	1 oz
Luncheon meats, 95% fat free	1 oz
Cheese, low fat cottage cheese	¼ cup
low fat cheese (less than 3 grams fat per oz)	1 oz

Beans (Count as one very lean meat and one starch exchange.)

Dried beans, peas, lentils and dal, cooked	½ cup

Medium and high fat meat and substitutes
One serving have 5-8 grams of fat and 75-100 calories.

Beef, most beef products fall in this category (5 grams fat)	1 oz
Pork (5–8 grams of fat)	1 oz
Lamb: rib, roast, ground (5 grams fat)	1 oz
Poultry: ground turkey or chicken with skin (5 grams fat)	1 oz
Cheese, low fat cheese (5 grams fat)	1 oz
Regular cheese, American, cheddar (8–9 grams of fat)	1 oz
Paneer, whole milk (8 grams fat)	¼ cup
Egg (limit 3 per week) (5 grams fat)	1
Tofu (5 grams fat)	½ cup
Processed meats such as regular luncheon meats, hot dogs, sausages, brats (8–9 grams fat)	1 oz
Peanut butter (8 grams of fat)	2 tbsp

Fats

One serving has 45 calories,
0 grams carbohydrate,
0 grams protein and
5 grams fat.

Polyunsaturated fats

Margarine	1 tsp
Oil, vegetable	1 tsp
Salad dressing, regular	1 tbsp
Salad dressing, reduced fat	2 tbsp
Nuts: almonds, cashews, mixed	6 nuts
Peanuts	10 nuts
Pecans, walnuts	2 whole
Seeds: sesame, pumpkin, sunflower	1 tbsp

Saturated fats

Butter	1 tsp
Coconut, fresh, grated	3 tbsp
Coconut, desiccated	1 tbsp
Coconut milk	1 tbsp
Coconut oil	1 tsp
Cream cheese	1 tbsp
Cream, whipping	1 tbsp
Half-and-half	2 tbsp
Sour cream	2 tbsp
Ghee	1 tsp

Free foods

One serving of *free food* has less than 20 calories or less than 5 grams of carbohydrate. Foods listed without a serving size can be used as desired. Foods listed with a serving size should be limited to three servings per day and spread out through the day.

Bouillon, broth, consomme
Carbonated or mineral water, club soda
Coffee, tea
Condiments such as horseradish, lemon juice, mustard, soy sauce, vinegar
Diet soft drinks, sugar free
Sugar free drink mixes, tonic water
Spices, all
Sugar free gelatin, gum
Sugar substitutes, aspartame, saccharin, acesulfame K

Ketchup, taco sauce	1 tbsp
Cocoa powder, unsweetened	1 tbsp
Jam or jelly, low sugar or light	2 tsp
Salsa	¼ cup
Sugar free hard candy	1 candy

Combination foods

Food	Serving Size	Exchange/Serving
Barfi, milk or khoa	1 × 2 inches	1 starch, 2 fat
Cake, brownie, unfrosted	2-inch square	1 starch, 1 fat
Chips, any	1 oz	1 starch, 2 fats
Cookies, 2 in. diameter	2 small	1 starch, 1 fat
French fried potatoes	10–12 (2 oz)	1 starch, 1 fat
Halwa	½ cup	2 starches, 2 fats
Ice cream	½ cup	1 starch, 2 fats
Ice cream, low fat	½ cup	1 starch, 1 fat
Kheer, whole milk	½ cup	1 milk, 1 starch, 2 fats
Kheer, low fat milk	½ cup	1 milk, 1 starch, 1 fat
Pizza: cheese, vegetarian, thin crust	¼ of 10 inch	2 starches, 2 medium fat meats, 1 fat
Pizza, meat topping	¼ of 10 inch	2 starches, 2 medium fat meats, 2 fats
Pudding, made with low fat milk	½ cup	2 starches
Pudding, sugar free	½ cup	1 starch
Samosa, potato	1 medium	1 starch, 1 fat
Soups: bean	1 cup	1 starch, 1 lean meat
Cream (made with water)	1 cup	1 starch, 1 fat
Tomato or vegetable	1 cup	1 starch

Sample meal plans using food exchanges

Here is a sample of how to distribute daily calorie intake to obtain adequate nutrition. Make sure to divide the total exchanges into three meals and a snack if needed. If you choose not to have a snack, distribute those exchanges equally at the other meals. The total exchanges are used to calculate the nutrient distribution. The exchanges are given on the previous pages. They provide great variety and balance in meal planning. The recommendations for a well-balanced meal plan are fat less than 30 percent, carbohydrate 50–70 percent and protein 10–20 percent. Be careful of serving sizes and avoid skipping meals.

1200 Calories
Fat: 33 grams (25%)
Carbohydrate: 170 grams (55%)
Protein: 62 grams (20%)

Exchange groups	Total	Breakfast	Lunch	Dinner	Snack
Starches	6	2	1	2	1
Fruits	3	1	1		1
Milk	2	1		1	
Vegetables	2–4		1–2	1–2	
Meats	4		2	2	
Fats	3	1	1	1	

1500 calories
Fat: 40 grams (25%)
Carbohydrate: 215 grams (55%)
Protein: 80 grams (20%)

Exchange groups	Total	Breakfast	Lunch	Dinner	Snack
Starches	8	2	2	3	1
Fruits	4	1	2		1
Milk	2	1		1	
Vegetables	2–4		1–2	1–2	
Meats	5		2	3	
Fats	4	1	1	2	

1800 calories
Fat: 50 grams (25%)
Carbohydrate: 245 grams (55%)
Protein: 85 grams (20%)

Exchange groups	Total	Breakfast	Lunch	Dinner	Snack
Starches	10	2	2	4	2
Fruits	4	1	2		1
Milk	2	1		1	
Vegetables	2–4		1–2	1–2	
Meats	6		2	4	
Fats	5	1	2	2	

2000 calories
Fat: 55 grams (25%)
Carbohydrate: 275 grams (55%)
Protein: 95 grams (20%)

Exchange groups	Total	Breakfast	Lunch	Dinner	Snack
Starches	12	3	3	4	2
Fruits	4	1	2		1
Milk	2	1		1	
Vegetables	2–4		1–2	1–2	
Meat	6		2	4	
Fats	6	2	2	2	

For *lactovegetarian* or *lacto-ovovegetarian* diets (see under Vegetarian meals on the next page) these distributions should work well. If the meat and substitute exchanges are too high, they can be reduced to 3–4 meat exchanges per day and substituted with any of the other exchanges except fat, without compromising nutrition. Eat a variety of foods within each exchange. Beans, lentils and pulses, when combined with other exchanges like grains or milk, provide a adequate amount and a variety of protein.

Vegetarian meals

Being a vegetarian was considered a fad not too long ago in the United States. As the health benefits of vegetarian diet are being recognized, it is becoming more acceptable. Health organizations like the American Heart Association recommend that individuals should consume no more than 6 ounces of meat per day; so more and more, people are looking for alternatives. Many are becoming vegetarians or substituting some vegetarian meals in their diets. In this country the variety in vegetarian meals is often limited.

As stated previously in India, vegetarian meals are a way of life. Approximately 30–40 percent of Indians are vegetarians. Even nonvegetarians in India do not eat meat every day or at every meal. Among Hindus, during auspicious and religious occasions, meat is usually not permitted. Indians have been vegetarians for centuries, and therefore the variety in vegetarian meals is virtually unlimited.

What is a vegetarian or a vegetarian diet?

A vegetarian is a person who eats no meat, poultry or fish. There are three main types of vegetarian diets. People often use the term vegetarian for all these types of diets.

Vegan: A strict vegetarian diet that excludes all animal products including eggs, milk and dairy products.

Lactovegetarian: A vegetarian diet that includes milk and milk products.

Lacto-ovovegetarian: A vegetarian diet that includes eggs, milk and milk products.

Most Indians are lactovegetarians. Milk, yogurt and buttermilk are used extensively in the meal preparation and planning. Eggs are becoming more acceptable in the Indian vegetarian diets. In the United States lacto-ovovegetarian diets are the most prevalent.

Nutritional adequacy of vegetarian diets

Indian vegetarian meals (lactovegetarian) if planned properly, provide most of the nutrients needed. Keep the following nutritional needs in mind to provide a healthy vegetarian diet.

- *Protein:* Protein is found in most plant foods. Indian meals use an abundant amount of dried beans, nuts, whole grains, vegetables and dairy products. Most of the time one or more of these food groups are included in any given meal. Vegetarians do not need to worry about combining foods as the old "complementary protein theory" advised. It was believed that protein from different vegetable sources must be combined in appropriate ways to obtain adequate high-quality protein, called complementary protein. The latest recommendations indicate that the body will make its own complete protein if a variety of foods and enough calories are eaten during the day.

- *Calcium:* Milk, yogurt and buttermilk are rich in calcium. Other good sources are dark leafy greens such as mustard greens, dried beans and jaggery.

- *Iron:* Good plant sources of iron include dried beans, dark green leafy vegetables, dried fruits, jaggery and fortified breads and cereals. Include foods rich in vitamin C (fruits, juices or tomatoes) along with iron-containing foods to increase iron absorption.

- *Vitamin B12:* Vitamin B12 is found in all foods of animal origin including eggs and dairy products; therefore, is not of concern in most Indian vegetarian diets.

- Choose a wide variety of foods to get all the nutrients you need. Select a variety among fruits, vegetables, dried beans and whole grains.

- Reduce fat intake by using low fat products and low fat cooking methods.

Indian vegetarian meals are unique in their composition and taste. Spices and the methods of preparation enhance the flavor of the food. Indian vegetarian meals are not limited to salads and steamed vegetables. Due to the varied tropical climate of India, the assortment of vegetables available are bounteous. As the ethnic population in this country increases, the variety of tropical vegetables and fruits available is also increasing. Many dried beans and grains are easily available in Indian or other ethnic stores. Those who are following a vegetarian diet or would like a vegetarian meal occasionally should try an Indian vegetarian meal for variety and pleasure.

A word about sodium

Sodium and salt are often used interchangeably, but they are not the same. Table salt is made up of sodium and chloride. Salt is the primary source of sodium in Indian diets. Sodium is an essential mineral, involved in almost all body functions including water balance, transmission of nerve impulses and maintaining normal muscle contractions.

Sodium and salt are found naturally in foods such as milk, meats and certain vegetables. Sodium adds flavor to foods such as breads, vegetables and prepared foods. Salt helps keep some foods safe by preserving them such as pickles, papads, chutneys and cheese.

The average adult consumes 4000–6000 mg of sodium per day. For people who do not have high blood pressure, the National Research Council recommends 2000–4000 mg of sodium or less per day.

The link between sodium intake and high blood pressure is unclear. A high sodium diet alone does not cause high blood pressure. A combination of factors can affect blood pressure including family history of high blood pressure, excess body weight, age, race, lack of physical activity and smoking. People whose blood pressure increases with higher intake of sodium are called "salt sensitive" and might benefit from reducing their intake of sodium. People with high blood pressure should consult with their physician.

The sodium content of each recipe is provided. Moderate amounts of salt is used in preparing dishes. Salt can be adjusted to taste and individual requirements. Those who are on low sodium diet should reduce or eliminate the added salt.

Time-saving tips

As a working mother I am always looking for ways to cut down on cooking time. I love cooking but like to spend as little time as I can in the kitchen. Since the majority of Indian cooking is done on the stove top, I am known to use all four burners at once. Over the years, I have learned some prepreparation techniques and have used some time-saving devices to significantly reduce preparation and cooking time. On weekdays I like to spend no more than 30–45 minutes for meal preparation. Since the evening meal is the only home-cooked meal most of us eat, this meal has to be both nutritious and satisfying.

- The most important step is to have the ingredients on hand. See stocking your pantry for Indian cooking on page for items to keep on hand. Indian cooking uses many dried ingredients that can be stored for a long time. For perishables I like to do my grocery shopping only once a week to save time as well as money.

- Cleaning and chopping vegetables can be time consuming. I usually do the whole package at one time and refrigerate portions in sealed plastic bags. If you do not have time or do not like to mess with chopping vegetables, many grocery stores now carry chopped vegetables, which are convenient and quick to use. The taste of fresh vegetables cannot be duplicated; spend a little extra on fresh vegetables and taste the difference. It is well worth the money and time.

- Frozen vegetables are a nice substitute for fresh vegetables. I especially like to use frozen peas, French-style green beans, mixed vegetables and spinach. Keep a fair supply of these vegetables in your freezer.

- Stock some canned vegetables. For a quick meal these can be very handy. I have included some recipes using canned beans and sauces.

- Keep a running grocery list and encourage family members to add items as needed. This is especially helpful if you have more than one cook in the house.
- Plan meals for the upcoming week and add ingredients to the shopping list.
- Double the recipes and freeze the extra for those days when nobody can or wants to cook. However, remember that not all things freeze well.

Have the butcher package meats in family size packages, or divide it into meal size portions and freeze them. I usually have the butcher skin the chicken and chop or grind the meat to my specifications. They will also debone and trim meat. Some places charge a little extra and some will do it at no extra charge. To me it is well worth the money as it saves a lot of time and mess.

- To skin a chicken, use a paper towel to pull the skin. If it is partially frozen it skins even easier.
- Buy chopped garlic and substitute for fresh.
- Substitute frozen ginger for fresh. To freeze ginger, purchase ⅛–¼ pound of fresh, tender ginger. Peel and grate or chop all the ginger. To grate ginger, grate with the grain to minimize the fiber that comes out. If you have an electric chopper, finely chop the ginger and freeze it. I usually divide the ginger into approximately 1 teaspoon portions, placing them on a plate lined with plastic wrap and then freezing it. When it is completely frozen, remove it from the plastic wrap and storing in a sealed plastic bag or container. It takes time initially but on a daily basis it saves a lot of time.
- Substitute frozen onion masala. See onion masala under Homemade spice blends on page. Using the frozen onion masala can save a significant amount of time without altering the taste of the prepared dish.
- Use time-saving appliances like a blender, food processor, food chopper, pressure cooker or rice cooker when possible.
- To prepare meals in less than 45 minutes, use menu items that do not take longer than 30 minutes to cook. Use these basic suggestions:

1. Prepare the ingredients for the recipes.

2. Start the item that takes longest to cook first. Once the item has been

mixed and is now ready to simmer, move it to the back burner as it continues to cook. For a vegetarian meal I am most likely to start the dal in the pressure cooker first. For nonvegetarian meals, start with the meat.

3. Start the next item and make it accordingly. With a little practice a complete meal for four to six people can be prepared in less than 45 minutes. Some recipes, however, take a long time and should be cooked when more time is available.

Using the pressure cooker

After a long day at work, cooking beans can be very time consuming, and it is virtually impossible to cook whole dals in time for dinner. In India cooking with a pressure cooker is very common; it is economical and it saves fuel and time. It cooks food three to ten times faster than ordinary cooking methods. I use it to cook dals as well as for many other things like boiling potatoes and steaming vegetables. My personal preference is a heavy aluminum 4- or 6-quart pressure cooker. Some basic rules for pressure cooking are the following:

1. Follow the safety rules in the instruction manual of your pressure cooker. A pressure cooker is safe when used properly, but it can be very dangerous if the safety rules are not followed.
2. Prepare foods according to the recipe. Be sure not to overfill the pressure cooker.
3. Place the pressure regulator on the vent pipe.
4. Heat on the medium to high setting until the pressure regulator attains a gentle rocking motion. The cooking time begins when the pressure regulator begins to rock gently. Lower the heat to maintain a slow, steady rocking motion and cook for the length of time indicated in the recipe. Remember, food cooks much faster in a pressure cooker.
5. Remove the pressure cooker from the burner. If I have time I let the pressure drop on its own by letting the pressure cooker cool at room temperature. This, of course, causes additional cooking and for some recipes that may be acceptable. If the instructions state cool cooker at once, cool the cooker under running cold water.
6. After the pressure has dropped completely, remove the pressure regula-

tor. Always remove the pressure regulator before opening the cover. DO NOT FORCE THE COVER OFF. Continue the cooling until the cover opens easily.

7. Lift the cover carefully at arm's length distance away because some steam may escape.

8. Again remember to follow all the safety rules and enjoy the time savings of a pressure cooker.

Spices and other ingredients

Most of the ingredients and spices listed below are available at any supermarket that carries a large selection of spices. However, certain ingredients are only available at a grocery stores that carry Indian or Asian groceries. These days special ingredients are readily available in most medium to large size towns as many Oriental stores and cooperative or health food stores carry the Indian spices and dried beans. If necessary to order by mail, see Mail order at the end of this section.

Spices and their blends add distinct flavor and taste to each dish. A recipe may call for whole or ground spice. The whole variety is usually more potent than its powdered form. Substituting the spices can alter the taste and character of the dish. If an ingredient is not available, omitting it may be the better choice.

A list of spices and other ingredients is given below with their description and common Hindi translations.

Asafetida (heeng): It is a dried gum resin from the root of a plant. It has a very distinct pungent smell. It has medicinal properties that help in digestion, reduce gas formation and are beneficial in other ways. It is generally used in beans, pulses and some vegetables. Asafetida, in its pure form, is available as a lump or a rock. A powdered form which is mixed with other ingredients that makes it easier to use is also available. It takes only a pinch of asafetida to add a lot of flavor; yet it can be omitted from ny recipe without altering the flavor significantly. Always store it in a separate air-tight container.

Bay leaves (tej patra): An aromatic herb, bay leaves are most-often used as whole leaves for seasoning, although it may be ground in some spice blends.

Beans, legumes and pulses: See Bean, legumes and pulses under recipe section.

Besan: See chickpea flour.

Black pepper (kali mirch): Black pepper is used extensively in Indian cooking. It is used as a whole peppercorn as well as ground black pepper.

Cardamom (elaichi): There are two different types of cardamoms used in Indian cooking—black pods and green pods. The bleached white cardamom pods are generally not used.

> *Large black cardamom pods:* They look like black beetles and have a deeper flavor than the green pods. I use them in my garam masala or whole in some recipes. If unavailable, they can be substituted with the green small cardamom pods.

> *Small green pods:* Indians frequently use the green cardamom pods for flavoring a variety of dishes and desserts. Crushed cardamom is often added to tea for flavor. The green pods are also used as an after-dinner breath freshener or just chewed any time for flavor.

> *Cardamom seeds:* The black seeds are removed from the cardamom pods. They may be used as whole seeds in some recipes, crushed for garnishing or finely ground for flavoring.

Cayenne pepper: See chilies.

Chickpea flour (besan): This is the flour of chana dal (see Beans, legumes and pulses under recipe section) and is very versatile. It can be used as a thickener, a batter or as a binding agent.

Chilies (mirch): A variety of chilies are used in Indian cooking. The chilies can range from mild to very hot. Most common chilies used in Indian cooking are cayenne peppers. You can eliminate or reduce the chilies in the recipe without compromising the taste significantly—the hotness of food is a personal preference.

> *Green chilies (hari mirch):* These are mild to very hot and are usually chopped and added to recipes. They can also be sliced or served whole in salads. The hottest part of the chilies is the seeds so remove the seeds to reduce the hot taste if desired. Handle chilies carefully as they can make the skin tingle and the eyes burn.

> *Dried red chilies (lal mirch):* Commonly known as cayenne pepper. The green chilies, when fully ripe, are bright red. Whole dried red chilies are sometimes used as a seasoning. Typically, ground red chilies are used as it adds the distinct hotness to food. It is sold as red chili powder in stores that carry Indian groceries or as cayenne pepper in supermarkets.

Cinnamon (dalchini): Cinnamon is used both finely ground or as sticks. The cinnamon sticks have a more-pronounced flavor than ground cinnamon.

Clarified butter (ghee): Ghee has a light caramel color and a distinct aroma and taste. It is made from butter or cream. The butter is cooked until all the moisture is evaporated and the solids settle on the bottom. The solids are removed and the pure ghee is strained from the top. Ghee will keep for several months at room temperature, which probably explains its popularity in ancient times. Unlike butter, ghee has a high smoking point that makes it easy to cook with, especially over the stove. Ghee is often used in Indian cooking. Like butter, the taste of ghee is unsurpassable. Ghee is high in saturated fat and should be used

.paringly. I do not use ghee for most of my cooking. I have used ghee for
a few of the recipes because of its irreplaceable taste and flavor. Ghee is
available in most grocery stores that carry Indian groceries, and it can also
be made at home.

To make homemade ghee, melt a pound of butter in a small skillet over
ow heat. Without stirring, gently simmer for 15-25 minutes until the
solids settle to the bottom and turn light brown. Watch frequently to avoid
burning. Cool and strain through a handkerchief or similar material. Store
in a air-tight container at room temperature.

Cloves (*laung*): Cloves have a distinct aroma. They are used as a
whole spice or ground in blend of spices like garam masala.

Coconut (*nariyal*): For many south Indian dishes, fresh coconut is
used. In north India dehydrated coconut is more-commonly used since
fresh coconut is not readily available. Whole (fresh and dehydrated)
coconut is also used for religious and auspicious ceremonies, and
presweetened coconut is not used in Indian recipes.

Fresh coconut: When buying fresh coconut, make sure it is
not moldy or cracked. Shake it to make sure it has plenty of
water in it. To break a coconut, hold the coconut over the sink in
one hand and hit around the center with a hammer. As the shell
cracks, the coconut water will come out. Consider saving that
water. It is not used in cooking but it is a very refreshing drink.
The coconut should break into two halves. Remove the coconut
meat with a butter knife. If it is too difficult to remove, put the
coconut in the oven at 350° F for a few minutes until the woody
shell contracts and releases the coconut meat.

Rinse the coconut in cold water. Now the coconut can be
peeled with a peeler if needed or grated directly. I usually grate
the whole coconut and freeze it. A hand grater or a food
processor can be used. The frozen grated coconut thaws easily
and can be used as needed.

Dehydrated or desiccated coconut: Desiccated
coconut is a dehydrated coconut that has been finely grated. It is

almost like sawdust. Desiccated coconut is mostly used for desserts, but it can be substituted for fresh coconut in some recipes for convenience.

Coriander (*dhania*): This is one of the most-common spices. Both the fresh leaves and the mature seeds are used.

Coriander seeds: White to yellowish brown coriander seeds are slightly smaller than a peppercorn. The whole seeds are used in some recipes, but it is usually used as a finely ground powder.

Coriander powder: This is a very commonly used spice. It adds flavor to as well as thickens curries. It is very important to have good coriander powder. When it gets too old, it looses its taste and flavor. I like to buy the seeds and grind my own coriander powder. Grind coriander seeds in a blender or a coffee grinder and store it in an air-tight jar.

Coriander leaves (*hara dhania*): These leaves are an aromatic herb that look similar to parsley but have a much more distinct flavor. They are usually sold in bunches as cilantro (Spanish name, it is also called Chinese parsley). They are used as garnish, flavoring, or in a side condiments (chutney).

Cumin seeds (*jeera*): These long brown seeds are used in multiple ways. The cumin seeds are the most-commonly used seasoning in north Indian dishes. For maximum flavor and taste the cumin seeds are dry-roasted or fried in oil.

Cumin powder: The raw cumin seeds are ground and used in some recipes as a seasoning. Cumin powder is readily available in most supermarkets.

Roasted cumin powder: The cumin seeds are roasted to a dark brown to black color, ground and then used as seasoning or garnish. The flavor and aroma of roasted cumin powder is

indispensable in many dishes. See recipe under Homemade spice blends on page.

Curry leaves (meetha neem): These highly aromatic leaves are used as seasoning for many dishes from south India. Fresh or dried curry leaves are now available here. The fresh leaves are generally sold on the stem; pull the leaves off the stem just before using to maintain the maximum flavor. If the fresh ones are not available, you can use the dried ones although they have less flavor.

Dal: See Beans, legumes and pulses under recipes.

Fennel seeds (saunf): These are long, yellowish brown seeds, which are used whole, crushed or ground. They have a mild flavor that lingers. They are often eaten as a breath freshener or a digestive aid.

Fenugreek seeds (methi): These small, reddish brown seeds have a pleasantly bitter flavor. They also have a strong, sweetish smell similar to that of burnt sugar. It takes just a few seeds to add a lot of flavor to any prepared dish.

Flour (atta): See Indian breads under recipe section.

Garam masala: This is a blend of dried spices that is combined and ground together for use as a seasoning. Garam masala has its own unique flavors depending on the combination of spices used. There are a variety of garam masala recipes available. It can be a potent spice blend that can alter the taste of a recipe significantly. I like to grind my own. It lasts for a long time if it is stored in an air-tight container. Often cooks or families will have their own personal recipe for this blend of spices. My family recipe for garam masala is provided for you. See recipe under Homemade spice blends on page. You can also buy prepared garam masala.

Ghee: See Clarified butter.

Ginger (adarak): Fresh ginger is used in many dishes for its mildly pungent flavor. It is also believed to help in digestion and is therefore used in many bean and vegetable recipes. Dried ginger (*sonth*) is also used, most often in some blend of spices like garam masala.

Jaggery (gur): This is raw sugar made most commonly from juices of sugar cane. If jaggery is not available, you can substitute dark brown sugar.

Mango powder (amchur): This powder is made from dried unripe sour mangoes. It is most-commonly used as a dried powder. Amchur adds a sweet-sourness to food. If unavailable, lemon juice can be substituted.

Mango pulp: Canned mango pulp is available at most grocery stores that carry Indian groceries. Mango pulp is made from variety of mangoes. My personal favorite for shakes and ice cream is one made with the Alfanso mango. Besides the convenience, the flavor and taste of mango pulp is usually good. In season when good mangoes are available, use them for shakes if desired.

Masala: Masala when translated means spices. The word masala is used very loosely. It might refer to one spice, a blend of spices, for example garam masala, or a blend of spices and other seasonings that are ground together to provide the base for many Indian sauces, for example onion masala. Masala can be wet or dry.

Mint (pudina): This aromatic herb is often used as a flavoring. Fresh mint is used to make chutneys and added as a flavoring or garnish to many dishes like cold appetizers, drinks and yogurt dishes. Dried mint can be substituted, if necessary.

Mustard seeds (rai): Mustard seeds are the most-commonly used seasoning in south Indian dishes. They are tiny, reddish brown to black seeds from a certain variety of mustard plant—smaller than the common yellow mustard seed and much less pungent. Mustard seeds are usually dry-roasted or fried in oil when used as seasoning. Mustard seeds are also ground and used, especially in pickles.

Onion seeds (kalonji): These small, black onion seeds have a earthy aroma. They are generally used for pickling. Occasionally they are used for flavoring vegetables or fish.

Red food coloring: It is sometimes used to add distinct color to food.

Saffron threads (kesar): They are orange-red dried stamens of the flower, used chiefly to color food to a golden yellow. Saffron threads also contribute a mild aromatic flavor to food. Saffron is usually expensive and therefore used mostly in desserts or for special occasions. If saffron is not available, substitute yellow food coloring in desserts, or turmeric in curries.

Sambhar powder: This is a blend of spices used in making sambhar. Like garam masala, families are partial to sambhar powder. See recipe under Homemade spice blends on page. Sambhar powder is available at stores that carry Indian groceries.

Silver foil (vark): Silver foil is used solely as a decoration on many sweets (desserts). It makes the sweets look very elegant. It is an edible shimmering foil made of pure silver. The vark is sold between sheets of paper and should be handled carefully. It does not add or change the flavor or taste in anyway. It can easily be omitted from the recipe. (Gold foil is also available, but it is rare and very expensive.)

Tamarind (imli): Tamarind is available either dried or as a concentrated liquid. It has an acidic, sweet taste. It is used to add sourness to food and is also made into condiments (chutneys). The dried tamarind is soaked in water to rehydrate and make into pulp. The pulp or the juice then is used in many recipes. The concentrated tamarind is convenient, but since it is so condensed it should be used sparingly.

Turmeric (haldi): Turmeric is typically used as a powder, mainly to color food to a golden yellow. It has a mild earthy flavor, and it is also a digestive and an antiseptic aid.

Mail order

Spices and other ingredients can be ordered by mail from the companies below.

Foods of India
121 Lexington Avenue
New York, NY 10016
(212)-683-4419

Kamdar Plaza
2646 West Devon
Chicago, IL 60659
(773) 338-8100

Indian Groceries and Spices
10633 West North Avenue
Milwaukie, WI 53226
(414) 771-3535

Bazaar of India
1810 University Avenue
Berkeley, CA 94703
(510) 548-4110

Homemade spice blends

Here are my recipes for the masalas. They are well worth the effort. Store them in a cool dry place in an air-tight container and they will last a long time. Good food begins with good masala!

Garam masala

This is my mothers recipe. I have a feeling it came through many generations. Garam masala is frequently used in my recipes. A coffee grinder or a blender can be used to grind the masala.

½ cup cumin seeds
⅓ cup whole black peppercorns
½ cup large cardamom pods
1 tbsp cloves
4 cinnamon sticks
10–12 bay leaves
1 tbsp dried ginger powder

1. Lightly dry-roast cumin seeds. Cool to room temperature.
2. Combine all the spices and grind to a fine powder. Sift the spices to eliminate any chunks.
3. Store in a air-tight container.

Makes about 1½ cups

Roasted cumin powder

Roasting cumin seeds brings out their full flavor. The powder is used for garnishing and flavoring many dishes.

¼ cup cumin seeds

1. In a fry pan or on an iron griddle (tava), dry-roast cumin seeds over medium heat until reddish brown to dark brown. Cool to room temperature.
2. Grind the seeds in a blender or spice grinder. Store in air-tight container.

Makes about ⅓ cup

Sambhar powder

Homemade sambhar powder has a much fresher taste than most store-bought ones. You can also control the hotness of the sambhar powder by seasoning with chilies to your taste.

4 tbsp chana dal
4 tbsp coriander seeds
1 tsp mustard seeds
1–3 dried red hot chilies
¼ tsp fenugreek seeds

1. In a small fry pan dry-roast the above spices on low heat until the chana dal is reddish brown.
2. Cool and grind the spices to a fine powder.
3. Store in a air-tight container.

Makes ¾ cup

Onion masala

Several of the recipes call for onions to be ground and fried. Making onion masala is a time-consuming and smelly proposition. For convenience I usually make and freeze onion masala ahead of time. Once the onions are cooked the smell is reduced significantly. It takes time initially but saves a lot of time later. Use a good exhaust when you make onion masala.

3 lb onions
½ cup oil

1. Peel onions, cut into 6–8 pieces. Grind the onions to a fine paste. A little bit of water (about 1–2 tbsp) might be needed to get the blender to work.
2. Pour into a large fry pan and cook over high heat until most of the water is evaporated, stirring occasionally.
3. Reduce heat to medium high, add oil and fry onions stirring constantly to avoid burning. Fry until the onions are light brown. The onions will draw away from the sides of the pan into a dense mass.
4. Cool to room temperature. I usually divide the onions into approximately 1 tbsp portions, place them on a plate lined with plastic wrap and freeze. When they are completely frozen, remove from the plastic wrap and store in a sealed plastic bag or container.

Note: Substitute 1 tbsp of frozen onion masala for 1 small onion, 1½ tbsp for a medium onion. Remember to reduce the oil by 2 teaspoons for every 1 tbsp of masala to compensate for the oil in the onion masala.

Makes about 1 cup

Kitchen equipment

Indian cooking does not take any special utensils. If you have a well-equipped kitchen you may not need anything special for authentic Indian cooking.

The equipment listed below helps save time, energy and fat in cooking.

Electric blender: A sufficiently powerful blender is very useful for grinding all kinds of masala (spices). In earlier days people used different types of stones for grinding.

Food processor or dough maker: A food processor is very helpful for grinding some dals or grains. I find a food processor or dough maker most useful for making all types of dough for variety of Indian breads.

Electric coffee grinder: The coffee grinder is the most-effective way of grinding spices in seconds. It grinds them finer than a blender, although a blender can be used followed by a sieve. Wipe the coffee grinder clean before storing. To avoid any problem of a spice smell lingering in the coffee grinder, wipe it clean immediately.

Electric food chopper: Although not necessary, it is nice for chopping onions, ginger or chilies in large quantity.

Electric rice cooker: If you frequently cook large quantities of rice, the electric rice cooker is useful. It allows for foolproof cooking of rice. Rice is not cooked any faster in a rice cooker but it is convenient to use.

Heavy skillets, pots and pans: Indian cooking requires browning (bhun-na) and seasoning (chounk) on the stove. A heavy bottom that allows for even cooking and can withstand long periods of heating is better suitable for Indian cooking, especially copper or aluminum bottoms or the newer vessels that are made of alloys.

Nonstick fry pans: Heavy nonstick fry pans are great as you need a lot less oil or fat for cooking. They are irreplaceable in the kitchen. Care to prevent ruining the finish. A good combination is a small one (6 inch) and a large (10 inch) one with lids for all types of cooking, especially vegetables.

Karhai or wok: An Indian karhai is similar to a wok. It is used mainly for frying and some roasting or browning. The karhai is usually small and made of heavy material, often cast iron. If you do not have a karhai, a wok or a fry pan can be substituted. Less oil is wasted in karhai, due to its construction versus that of an electric fryer. An electric wok is not suitable for most Indian frying although the electric fryer can be used for some of the frying.

Pressure cooker: A pressure cooker saves time and energy. It is irreplaceable for cooking beans. See using pressure cooker under Time-saving tips on page.

Iron skillet (tava): A cast-iron, slightly rounded or flat surface is best for cooking chapati or roti. It maintains temperature and allows for even cooking. A heavy fry pan can be substituted for tava.

Methods of preparation

Indian cuisine is unique in its methods of preparation. Most Indian cooking is done on the stove top, using direct heat. A clay underground oven (tandoor) is used for some cooking in the Punjab region. A gas or electric oven can be substituted for tandoor.

Basic Indian food is a blend of spices, seasonings and flavorings to bring out the unique taste, flavor and aroma of each food. Because of all the form of spice (whole, ground or roasted) and the methods of preparation (roasting, in a sauce or fried) the array of possible foods is endless. When our friends get together and of course have something to eat, the conversation often turns to food. I am always amazed at how many different ways we prepare the same vegetable. My friends from east or south India will often prepare the same vegetable with a totally different medium than people from the north. The combining of different vegetables or dals will also change the taste or texture of food.

Curry is often misinterpreted to be anything that looks yellow or resembles Indian food. The so-called "curry" to me is the gravy or the sauce the food is in. We call it *rasa*. Flour is rarely used as a thickener in Indian cooking. Spices, garlic, onion, yogurt or tomatoes are used to flavor and thicken the sauce or rasa. All Indian foods are not in a curry sauce; many foods are spiced yet have no liquid.

Some common methods of preparation are described below.

Chounk (seasoning): This is the most-common way to season the food. Oil or ghee is heated until it is very hot and a slight film develops over the oil. Spices like cumin or mustard seeds are dropped into the hot oil and cooked for only a few seconds until the seeds begin to brown, pop or change color. This seasoned oil is the chounk. One may add the hot seasoned oil to the food or add the food to the seasoned oil. The chounk enhances the flavor of the spices and the food.

Bhun-na (roasting): Roasting or browning of spices and food is another very common method of bringing out the taste and flavor. The food or spices may be dry-roasted or roasted in hot oil.

> *Dry-roasting:* For dry-roasting, heat the ingredients in a heavy fry pan over low to medium high heat, stirring or shaking the pan occasionally. This roasting procedure really brings out the flavor of the spice. For example cumin seeds are dry-roasted and ground for seasoning uncooked food like yogurt.

> *Roasting in oil:* Spices are added to hot oil and browned before other ingredients are added for cooking. They may also be added to this seasoned oil and browned before the water is added to make the sauce (rasa). I remember my mother saying the more you "bhuno" it, the better the flavor.

Thickening the sauce (rasa): If the sauce or rasa is too thin, remove the lid of the pan, increase the heat and allow the liquid to evaporate to the desired consistency. This is often done for sauce with varied consistency. Actually thickening also adds to the flavor of the dish. When cooking a dry vegetable (sukhi subji), even if no water is added, the water from the vegetable is leached out. Once the vegetable is cooked to the desired tenderness, the liquid is evaporated and the spices cling to the food.

Adding yogurt to the masala: Yogurt is added to many sauces to give them a creamy texture as well as thickening and adding slight tartness to food. Yogurt curdles when it is heated. To avoid curdling, lightly whip the yogurt to break any lumps. Add one tablespoon at a time to the browning sauce or masala. Fry or "bhuno" the masala until the yogurt is fully absorbed before adding the next tablespoon.

Making it low fat: As mentioned earlier the spices and food is seasoned (*chounk*) and roasted (*bhun-na*) in oil. To maintain the authentic flavor and texture of food, start with roasting the spices in very small amount of oil. Then add the food and roast it if needed. (Using a nonstick pan helps if more roasting is to be done.) Once the food is cooked, remove the lid and reduce the sauce (rasa) to the desired consistency. For foods with sauce, there is no need to add more oil. For dry vegetables that have to be roasted in oil, first cook the vegetables and evaporate the liquid, if any. Then add a small amount of oil and roast (*bhuno*) some more to bring the desired full flavor and texture. The total amount of fat in the prepared dish is significantly less than the original recipe without compromising any of the taste.

Stocking the pantry for Indian cooking

Start with the ingredients for particular recipes and build the pantry.

Spices and flavorings

For detailed information, see Spices and other ingredients on page 44-52.

Asafetida (*heeng*)
Bay leaves (*tej patra*)
Cardamom (*elaichi*)
    Black large cardamom
    Green cardamom
Chilies (*mirch*)
    Cayenne pepper
    Dried whole red chilies
Cinnamon (*dal chini*)
Coconut (*nariyal*)
    Fresh coconut
    Dehydrated or desiccated coconut
Coriander (*dhania*)

Coriander seeds

Coriander powder

Cumin seeds (*jeera*)

Cumin powder

Roasted cumin powder

Curry leaves (*meetha neem*)

Fennel seeds (*saunf*)

Garam masala

Garlic (*lehsun*)

Jaggery (*gur*)

Mango powder (*amchur*)

Mustard seeds (*rai*)

Saffron threads (*kesar*)

Sambhar powder

Silver foil (*vark*)

Tamarind (*imli*)

Turmeric (*haldi*)

Dals:

For detailed information, see beans, legumes and pulses on page 146.

Bengal gram (Chana dal)

Black-eyed peas (*lobhia*)

Black gram, whole *(sabut urd)*

  Dehusked *urd (dhuli)*

Chickpeas (*kabuli chana*)

Kidney beans (*rajmah*)

Lentils (*masoor*)

Moong beans, whole (*sabut moong*)
  Split moong
  Dehusked moong (*dhuli moong dal*)
Pigeon peas (*toor dal*)

Canned foods

Black-eyed peas
Chickpeas (garbanzo beans)
Kidney beans
Light fruit
Mango pulp
New potatoes
Tomato sauce

Flour, rice and miscellaneous

Basmati rice
Chickpeas flour (*besan*)
Clarified butter (*ghee*)
Cream of rice
Cream of wheat (*sooji*)
Long grain rice
Red food coloring
Vegetable oil
White flour
Whole wheat flour *or*
  Durum wheat flour (*atta*)

Dairy

Butter
Low fat ricotta cheese
Margarine
Milk
Nonfat or low fat plain yogurt

Fresh vegetables

Eat 2–3 vegetables per day. Buy some fresh vegetables for cooking and some for salads.

Cauliflower
Cabbage
Celery
Cucumber
Eggplant
Fresh coriander leaves (cilantro)
Fresh ginger (*adarak*)
Fresh mint
Gourds, seasonal
Green beans
Green chilies
Green peppers
Lettuce
Okra
Onions
Potatoes
Radishes
Spinach
Tomatoes

Winter squashes
Zucchini

Fresh fruit

Have enough fruit to last the family for one week. Canned and dried fruits are a good substitute when or if fresh fruit is finished or not available.

Banana
Apples
Seasonal fruits

Meat, poultry and seafood

(Fresh or frozen)

Chicken
Fish
Lamb
    Cubed lamb
    Ground lamb
    Lamb chops
Shrimp

Frozen foods

Mixed vegetables
Mustard greens, chopped
Peas
Spinach, chopped

Menus

Some menu suggestions for nonvegetarian meals, vegetarian meals and special occasions are given below. Use the appropriate serving size to meet your caloric needs.

Indian meals are usually eaten with chapati (roti) and/or rice. Papad, salad, chutney, pickles, plain yogurt or raita are often served as condiments or side dishes. Add to your meals as desired.

Nonvegetarian menus (two weeks)

Tandoori murgh (barbecued chicken)
Alu matar (potato and pea curry)
Piaz aur tamatar ka salad (onion and tomato salad)
Naan/rice

Murgh sabji wala (chicken with vegetables)
Rice

Murgh tari (chicken curry)
Phul gobhi salad (stir-fried salad)
Rice/naan

Mysore murgh (stir-fried chicken)
Alu raita (yogurt with potatoes)
Salad
Roti/rice

Murgh sag wala (chicken with spinach)
Tamatar piaz ka raita (yogurt with tomatoes and onion)
Rice

Machhi kali mirch (baked fish with black pepper)
Bengun (eggplant with tomatoes and onion)
Kheere ka raita (yogurt with cucumber)
Rice

Machhi aur ghia (fish with zucchini)
Rice

Sarson wali machhi (fish in a mustard sauce)
Bean-moong ki subji (French-style green beans)
Rice

Machhi tari (fish curry)
Gobhi-gajar salad (cabbage and carrot salad)
Rice

Tamatari jhinga (shrimp with tomatoes)
Sukhi matar (spicy peas)
Rice

Lamb kalia (chopped spicy lamb)
Alu gobhi (potatoes with cauliflower)
Roti/rice

Alu gosht (lamb with potatoes)
Piaz aur tamatar ka salad (onion and tomato salad)
Tahari (vegetable rice)

Rogan josh (lamb in yogurt sauce)
Bandh gobhi (cabbage and peas)
Rice

Madrasi gosht (chopped lamb)
Palak alu (spinach and potatoes)
Neembu chawal (lemon rice)

Kheema (ground lamb with peas)
Gobhi gajar ki subji (cauliflower and mixed vegetables)
Roti/rice

Vegetarian menus (two weeks)

Toor dal (pigeon peas)
Gajar ki subji (sweet-and-sour carrots)
Roti/rice

Masoor dal (lentil soup)
Bandh gobhi (cabbage and peas)
Rice/roti

Chana dal aur lauki (chana dal with celery)
Bhindi tamatar ki subji (okra with tomatoes)
Alu raita (yogurt with potatoes)
Roti/rice

Sprouted moong
Tamatar piaz ka raita (yogurt with tomatoes and onions)
Rice

Gujrati dal (sweet-and-sour dal)
Bengun (eggplant with tomatoes and onions)
Kheere ka raita (yogurt with cucumbers)
Rice/roti

Sambhar (toor dal with vegetables)
Nariyal chutney (coconut chutney)
Idli (steamed rice dumplings)

Kaddi (chickpeas soup)
Jeera alu (spicy new potatoes)
Piaz aur tamatar ka salad (onion and tomato salad)
Rice

Sukhi moong dal (dry moong dal)
Kele ka raita (yogurt with banana)
Palak alu (spinach and potatoes)
Rice

Rajmah (kidney beans)
Alu ka raita (yogurt with potatoes)
Cachumber (tomato, cucumber, onion salad)
Rice

Sukha lobhia (black-eyed peas)
Alu matar (potato and pea curry)
Rice

Subji biriyani (vegetable-rice casserole)
Kheere ka raita (yogurt with cucumber)

Alu matar (potato and pea curry)
Paneer ke naan (cheese-stuffed naan)

Matar pulao (rice pilaf with peas)
Dhania chutney (coriander chutney)
Dahi (plain yogurt)
Chana-rajmah salad (mixed bean salad)

Missi roti (chickpea flour roti)
Phul gobhi salad (stir-fried salad)
Lassi (yogurt drink)

Menus for special occasions

Nonvegetarian and vegetarian special occasion menus are given.

Dal makhani (whole urd dal)
Bharwa hari mirch (stuffed bell peppers)
Cachumber (tomato, cucumber, onion salad)
Dhania chutney (coriander chutney)
Rice/coiled roti
Kheer (rice pudding)

Chole (spicy chickpeas)
Alu gobhi (potatoes with cauliflower)
Piaz aur tamatar ka salad (onion and tomato salad)
Naan/rice

Rajmah (kidney beans)
Bhindi tamar ki subji (okra with tomatoes)
Dahi pakori (moong bean balls)
Imli chutney (tamarind chutney)
Rice
Mango ice cream

Tandoori jhinga (fish curry)
Sprouted moong
Alu matar (potato and pea curry)
Kheere ka raita (yogurt with cucumber)
Rice
Nariyal Barfi (diamond-shaped coconut sweet)

Seekh kebobs (barbecued lamb on skewers)
Bengun (eggplant with tomatoes and onion)
Kheere ka raita (yogurt with cucumber)
Pudina chutney (mint chutney)
Tandoori alu roti (potato-stuffed roti)

Matar paneer (pea and cheese curry)
Mughlai murgh (chicken with almonds and raisins)
Phul gobhi salad (stir-fried salad)
Rice/roti
Gajar halwa (carrot sweet)

Palak paneer (spinach with cheese)
Tandoori murgh (barbecued chicken)
Bhuna chawal (roasted rice)
Kulfi (Indian ice cream)

Spices

See page 44

1. Mango powder
2. Cumin seeds
3. Coriander powder
4. Cayenne pepper
5. Garam masala
6. Turmeric
7. Salt
8. Coriander seeds
9. Onion seeds
10. Bay leaves
11. Chana dal
12. Fennel seeds
13. Black cardamom
14. Mustard seeds
15. Dried red chilies
16. Cardamom
17. Fenugreek seeds
18. Cloves
19. Black peppercorn
20. Cinnamon sticks
21. Tamarind

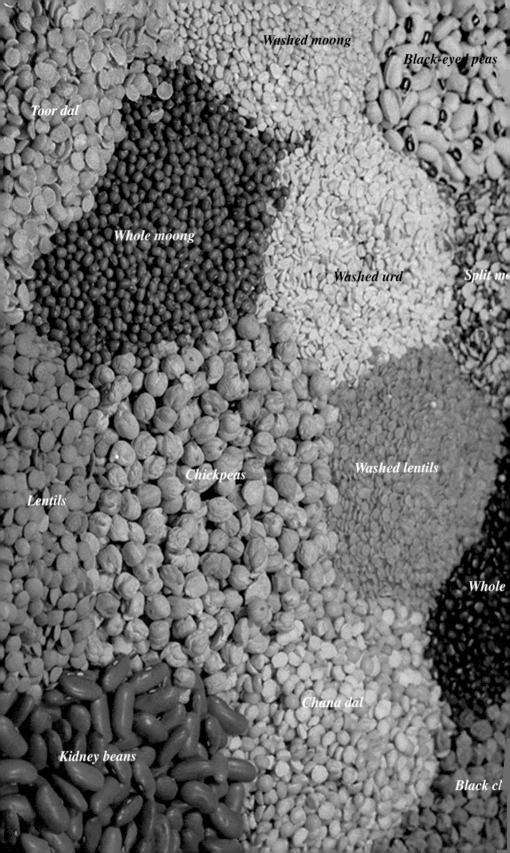

Toor dal

Washed moong

Black-eyed peas

Whole moong

Washed urd

Split m

Chickpeas

Washed lentils

Lentils

Whole

Kidney beans

Chana dal

Black cl

Samosa (Potato-stuffed pastry): Page 106

Poha (Pounded rice snack): Page 102

Bharva hari mirch (Stuffed bell peppers): Page 180

Chole (Spicy chickpeas): Page 170

Matar pulao (Rice pilaf with peas): Page 132

Jeera alu (Spicy new potatoes): Page 175

Bhindi tamatar ki sabji *(Okra): Page 188*

Bengun (Eggplant): Page 192

Gobhi gajar ki sabji (Cauliflower): Page 176

Murgh sabji wala (Chicken): Page 216

Bean-moong ki sabji (Green beans): Page 196

Bund gobhi (Cabbage and peas): Page ▌

Sprouted moong: Page 152

Machhi aur ghia (Fish/zucchini): Page 2▌

Matar paneer (Peas and cheese curry): Page 200

ıbhar (Toor dal with vegetables): Page 168   *Idli (Steamed rice dumplings): Page 140*

Machhi kali mirch (Baked fish with black peppers): Page 229

Rogan josh (Lamb in yogurt sauce): Page 246

Tandoori murgh
Barbecued chicken
Page 212

Gajar Halwa (Carrot halwa): Page 284

Nariyal barfi (Coconut sweets): Page 287

Recipes

Metric conversions*

Approximate conversions are given below. All conversions are based on level measurements.

Abbreviations

Throughout the book the following abbreviations have been used:

tsp	teaspoon
tbsp	tablespoon
oz	ounce
gm	gram
cm	centimeter
ml	milliliter

Weights

1 oz	28 gm
2 oz	57 gm
4 oz (¼ lb)	114 gm
6 oz	170 gm
8 oz (½ lb)	227 gm
12 oz	340 gm
16 oz (1 lb)	454 gm
32 oz (2 lb)	908 gm
2.2 lb	1 kg

Volume

⅛ tsp	½ ml
¼ tsp	1 ml
½ tsp	2 ml
1 tsp	5 ml
2 tsp	10 ml
1 tbsp	15 ml
¼ cup (4 tbsp)	60 ml
⅓ cup	80 ml
½ cup	120 ml
⅔ cup	160 ml
¾ cup	180 ml
1 cup	240 ml
4 cups (1 quart)	940 ml
4¼ cup	1 liter

Linear measurements

½ inch	1 cm
1 inch	2.5 cm
6 inches	15 cm
8 inches	20 cm

Temperatures

Fahrenheit	Celsius
350	175
375	190
400	205
425	220
450	230

* Figures calculated by 1 oz =28.35 gm; 1 lb= 454 gm; 2.2 lbs = 1 kg; 1 tbsp = 14.8 ml; 1 cup = 237 ml; 1 inch = 2.54 cm.

Beverages and snacks

Water is the beverage of choice in India. Water is served with all meals as it is cool and soothing and tastes best with all Indian foods.

Tea is served at any time, most-commonly at breakfast and tea time, which is around 5:00 p.m. Coffee is very popular in south India. A whole array of snacks are made to be served at tea time. Indians love to stop for tea and order a plate of samosas (potato-stuffed pastries). There are cafes that serve many beverages such as tea, expresso coffee, lassi and milkshakes with snacks all day. The variety of snacks are virtually unlimited. Snacks or savories are often fried and served with chutneys.

I have included a sampling of popular snacks and beverages in this chapter. Since tea time does not work into the schedule in this country, I serve several of the snacks as appetizers, a side dish or a light meal. Occasionally I serve dhokla with sambhara, uppama with a mango shake or samosa and dahi vada as a meal.

The snacks chosen for this book are lower in fat and high in taste. Enjoy them as light meals or any time of the day.

Chai
Indian tea

People have a passion for tea in India. Tea seems to lift the spirit at any time of the day. Tea time is 5:00 p.m. and usually includes snacks. It is an excellent way to wind up the workday. Tea in India is commonly served with milk and sugar. Spices are added, as desired, for flavor.

1 cup water
2 tbsp skim milk
1 cardamom pod*, crushed with mortar and pestle
1 tsp tea leaves or 1 tea bag
sugar to taste

1. Pour water and milk into a small saucepan. Add crushed cardamom pod. Bring to a boil. Reduce heat to simmer, and add tea leaves. Simmer for 1 minute. Remove from the heat. Let sit for 1–2 minutes.
2. Strain the tea into a cup. Add sugar or artificial sweetener if desired.

Makes 1 serving
Serving size: 1 cup
Amount per serving:

Exchanges: free

Calories 11	Carbohydrate . . . . 2 g
Fat .0 g	Dietary fiber . . . . 0 g
Saturated fat . . . . .0 g	Protein . . . . 1 g
Cholesterol . . . . .0 g	Sodium . . . . .22 mg

Variations: 1. Add ¼-inch fresh ginger, crushed with rolling pin, in the water. It is especially good in the winter or when you have a cold.
2. Some people also like cloves, cinnamon or black pepper in their tea. Use sparingly, adding to the water as other spices.

---

* If you make more than 1 cup of tea you don't necessarily need more spices. For example, I would add 1 cardamom pod for 1–3 cups of tea. The longer you let the spices boil in the water, more the flavor will come through.

Lassi

Yogurt drink

Sweet lassi is a very popular drink, especially on a hot summer day. It has a mild and refreshing flavor. Serve it with snacks or with a light lunch of poha or uppama.

⅔ cup nonfat plain yogurt
⅔ cup cold water
1 tbsp sugar
2–3 ice cubes

1. Place all the ingredients in a blender. Blend until frothy.
2. Pour into a tall glass and serve immediately.

Makes 1 serving
Serving size: 1½ cups
Amount per serving:

Exchanges: 1 milk
½ starch

Calories 130	Carbohydrate . . . . 24 g
Fat . . . . 0 g	Dietary fiber . . . . 0 g
Saturated fat . . . . 0 g	Protein . . . . 9 g
Cholesterol . . . . 3 g	Sodium . . . . 117 mg

Sugar free lassi

To make sugar free lassi substitute artificial sweetener for sugar.

Makes 1 serving
Serving size: 1½ cups
Amount per serving:

Exchange: 1 milk

Calories 85	Carbohydrate . . . . 12 g
Fat . . . . 0 g	Dietary fiber . . . . 0 g
Saturated fat . . . . 0 g	Protein . . . . 10 g
Cholesterol . . . . 3 g	Sodium . . . . 117 mg

Namkeen lassi
Buttermilk

Lassi is often made with salt and roasted cumin seeds to give it a delicate flavor. This taste is very similar to buttermilk. Actually, it is often made with fresh buttermilk in India.

⅔ cup nonfat plain yogurt
⅔ cup cold water
⅛ tsp salt
pinch of roasted cumin seed powder*

1. Place all the ingredients in a bowl and whip with a wire whip. Blend until smooth.
2. Pour into a tall glass and serve immediately.

Makes 1 serving
Serving size: 1½ cup
Amount per serving:

Calories	85	Carbohydrate	12 g
Fat	0 g	Dietary fiber	0 g
Saturated fat	0 g	Protein	9 g
Cholesterol	3 g	Sodium	370 mg

Exchange: 1 milk

---

* See recipe Roasted cumin powder on page 54.

Cold coffee

On hot summer days cold coffee is very refreshing.

2 tsp instant coffee
¼ cup hot water
2 cups skim milk
3 tbsp sugar
4–6 ice cubes

1. Mix coffee in hot water. Cool to room temperature.
2. In a blender jar combine cooled coffee, milk, sugar and ice cubes. Whip until frothy. Serve immediately.

Makes 2 servings
Serving size: 1½ cups
Amount per serving:

Exchanges: 1 milk
*   1 starch*

Calories	154	Carbohydrate	30 g
Fat	0 g	Dietary fiber	0 g
Saturated fat	0 g	Protein	8 g
Cholesterol	4 g	Sodium	126 mg

Sugar free cold coffee

To make sugar free cold coffee, substitute artificial sweetener for sugar.

Makes 2 servings
Serving size: 1½ cups
Amount per serving:

Exchange: 1 milk

Calories	86	Carbohydrate	12 g
Fat	0 g	Dietary fiber	0 g
Saturated fat	0 g	Protein	8 g
Cholesterol	4 g	Sodium	126 mg

Mango shake

In India a mango shake is made with milk instead of ice cream. I remember drinking this shake in the summer when mangoes were plentiful. I use canned mango pulp here because good mangoes suited for shakes are usually not available and it is convenient and available year round.

2 cups skim milk
⅔ cup mango pulp
2 tbsp sugar
4–6 ice cubes

In blender combine all ingredients and whip until frothy. Serve immediately.

Makes 2 servings
Serving size: 1½ cups

Exchanges: 1 milk
     1 fruit
     1 starch

Amount per serving:

Calories	199	Carbohydrate	41 g
Fat	0 g	Dietary fiber	2.4 g
Saturated fat	0 g	Protein	9 g
Cholesterol	4 g	Sodium	128 mg

Sugar free mango shake

To make sugar free mango shake substitute artificial sweetener for sugar.

Makes 2 servings
Serving size: 1½ cups

Exchanges: 1 milk
     1 fruit

Amount per serving:

Calories	154	Carbohydrate	30 g
Fat	0 g	Dietary fiber	2.4 g
Saturated fat	0 g	Protein	9 g
Cholesterol	4 g	Sodium	128 mg

Papad

Bean wafers

Many varieties of papad are available—they are plain, mild or spicy hot. Papad can be served with a meal, very much like potato chips, or eaten as a snack. Most papad are made from processed dals but there are also potato papad, rice papad and other sorts. The ones made with dals are the most common. If served as a snack, they are usually fried: if served with a meal, they are often roasted. I usually microwave my papad for convenience.

Papad made with dal are available at stores that carry Indian groceries.

Papad can be roasted in two different ways.

Direct fire: Roast papad one at a time on a gas or electric stove. On electric stove use a wire rack. Using tongs roast papad, turning frequently to avoid burning, until it puffs.

Microwave: Place one papad on a paper towel or a microwave-safe plate. Microwave each papad for 40–60 seconds on high (time will vary depending on the microwave power). The papad will puff evenly.

Makes 1 papad　　　　　　　　　*Exchange: ½ starch*
Serving size: 1 papad
Amount per serving:

Calories	35	Carbohydrate	6 g
Fat	0 g	Dietary fiber	2.5 g
Saturated fat	0 g	Protein	2.5 g
Cholesterol	0 g	Sodium	237 mg

Chivra
Snack mix

*Hot spicy snacks are very popular in India. The variety is unlimited.
Here is a quick and easy version using several available cereals.*

1½ cup corn flakes
1 cups crisped rice cereal
1 cup puffed corn cereal
1 tbsp vegetable oil
¼ tsp mustard seeds
½ cup mixed nuts
⅛ tsp cayenne pepper
¼ tsp salt
¼ tsp black pepper
¼ tsp mango powder

1. Combine cereal and set aside.
2. Heat oil in a large skillet. Add mustard seeds to hot oil and cover with a
   lid to avoid splattering. Fry for a few seconds until mustard seeds stop
   popping. Reduce heat to low. Add cereal mix and stir well. Add nuts,
   cayenne pepper, salt, black pepper and mango powder. Stir occasionally
   and roast for about 5–7 minutes. Remove from the heat and cool
   completely.
3. Store in air-tight container.

Makes 8 servings (4 cups)   *Exchanges: 1 starch*
Serving size: ½ cup   *1 fat*
Amount per serving:
Calories 110   Carbohydrate . . . . 11 g
Fat .7 g   Dietary fiber . . . . 1 g
Saturated fat . . . . .1 g   Protein . . . . 2 g
Cholesterol . . . . .0 g   Sodium . . . . .191 mg

Subji cutlets
Vegetable cutlets

The word cutlet has become part of the Indian language. Cutlets are a little work but they are well worth the effort. Serve them as an appetizer, snack or a side dish. I like to eat them with coriander chutney and kids like them with ketchup.

4 medium potatoes (1½ lb)
½ cup peas
½ cup chopped carrots, ¼-inch cubes
½ cup chopped green beans, ¼-inch pieces
1½ tsp salt
1 tbsp coriander powder
½ tsp cayenne pepper
1 tsp mango powder
1 tsp garam masala
2 tbsp chopped coriander leaves (cilantro)
¼ cup bread crumbs
⅓ cup vegetable oil

1. Boil potatoes. To avoid potatoes from getting sticky, remove from boiling water as soon as they are done and cool completely.
2. Steam chopped vegetables until tender, about 5 minutes. Cool to room temperature.
3. Peel and coarsely mash potatoes. Add steamed vegetables.
4. Add salt, coriander powder, cayenne pepper, mango powder, garam masala and chopped coriander leaves. Mix with your hands.
5. Shape mixture in to 1-inch × 2-inch oval patties.
6. Roll in bread crumbs.
7. Heat heavy skillet on medium heat. Add 1 tbsp oil and coat pan.

8. Place 8–10 cutlets in single layer. Pan-fry on medium heat for 7–10 minutes. Turn over and fry the other side. Add 1 tbsp oil moving the pan to allow even coating. Cutlets should be golden brown.
9. Repeat until all cutlets are done.
10. Serve immediately or reheat before serving. The cutlets can be served with ketchup or a variety of chutneys.

Makes 12 servings (24 cutlets)
Serving size: 2 cutlets
Amount per serving:

		Exchanges: 1 starch	
		1 fat	
Calories	103	Carbohydrate	11 g
Fat	6 g	Dietary fiber	1 g
Saturated fat	0.5 g	Protein	1 g
Cholesterol	0 g	Sodium	282 mg

Dahi pakori
Moong bean balls

This dish is served as a snack or a side dish. In northern India it is served with sweet-and-sour tamarind chutney as a "chat" (type of dishes that are typically spicy hot with some type of sweet-and-sour sauce). I like it hot and sour with lots of cayenne pepper and tamarind chutney. My friends from southern India serve it without chutney, as a side dish. This is a mouth-watering, healthy dish.

¾ cup washed moong dal
⅓ cup cold water
2½ tsp salt
vegetable oil for frying
2½ cups nonfat yogurt
½ cup skim milk
½ tsp roasted cumin seed powder*
¼–½ tsp cayenne pepper

1. Clean moong dal of any extraneous materials. Wash in 3–4 changes of water. Cover with water and soak overnight.
2. Place soaked dal in a strainer and rinse with cold water. Drain well. Place in a blender with ⅓ cup water and grind to a smooth paste. The paste will become light and fluffy. To test the batter, get a cup of cold water and with a finger-tip drop a small amount of batter into the water. The batter should float to the top. If it does not float, blend a little longer and repeat the process. When the batter floats to the top, empty into a bowl and mix in ½ tsp of salt. Set aside.
3. In a medium fry pan or *karhai* heat oil (only 1 inch deep) on high heat. When oil is very hot, make pakories (bean balls). Using a teaspoon or

---

* See recipe Roasted cumin powder on page 54.

finger-tips add about 1 heaping teaspoon of batter at a time to the oil. Add as many balls as the fry pan will hold in a single layer. Fry on one side until light brown, turn over and fry the other side until light brown, about 5 minutes on each side. Drain with slotted spoon and transfer to a paper towel lined plate. Repeat the process until all the batter is used. Set pakories aside. *

4. In medium bowl of very hot water add 1 tsp salt and mix. Add the pakories. Soak for 20–30 minutes.

5. In a medium bowl, whip yogurt, milk and 1 tsp salt.

6. Remove pakories from the soaking water by lightly squeezing 2–4 pakories between the palms of your hands. Take care not to break the pakories. Add the squeezed pakories to the yogurt. Discard the soaking water. Let stand at room temperature for 20 minutes or longer.

7. Before serving, garnish with roasted cumin seed powder and cayenne pepper. Serve with tamarind chutney (see recipe on page 275) if desired.

Makes about 30 pakories
Serving size: ⅛ recipe
Amount per serving:

Exchanges: 1 starch
1 lean meat

Calories 120	Carbohydrate . . . . 17 g
Fat . . . . 1.5 g	Dietary fiber . . . . 1 g
Saturated fat . . . . .0 g	Protein . . . . 9 g
Cholesterol . . . . .0 g	Sodium . . . . .467 mg

The pakories can be refrigerated or frozen for convenience. If frozen, thaw and use boiling hot water for soaking.

Dhokla

Steamed rice and bean cakes

This is a very popular dish from the state of Gujarat. It is served as a snack or a side dish, usually with coconut chutney or tamarind chutney. I like it with a cabbage and carrot vegetable dish (sambhara) for lunch or as a light dinner.

½ cup chana dal
½ cup long grain rice
½ cup water
¼ cup nonfat yogurt
1 tsp salt
⅛ tsp turmeric
1 green chili, chopped (optional)
1 tsp fresh ginger, chopped
½ tsp Eno*
1 tbsp vegetable oil
pinch of asafetida
½ tsp mustard seeds
6–8 curry leaves
1 tbsp fresh coriander, chopped
1 tbsp fresh grated coconut (optional)

1. Clean dal and rice of any extraneous materials. Wash in 3–4 changes of water. Cover with water and soak overnight.
2. Drain dal and rice, discarding the water. Place dal, rice, ½ cup water, yogurt, salt, turmeric, chili and ginger into a blender jar. Grind to a fine paste.

---

* Eno is usually available in Indian grocery stores. Use baking soda in equal portions if Eno is not available.

3. Place in a medium bowl and cover with a lid. Keep in a warm place for 12–24 hours. (I usually put it in the oven. To speed the process I sometimes turn on the oven light for a few hours.) The dough will ferment and start to rise.
4. Use a large saucepan with a tight lid that can fit a round or square metal cake pan. Brush or spray cake pan with oil. Place 1 cup water to a boil in the saucepan.
5. Add Eno to the fermented mixture and stir very gently from top to bottom, using a folding motion. Immediately transfer the mix into the cake pan, spreading the mix evenly.
6. Once the water is boiled, place the cake pan in the water using tongs and cover with a lid, reduce heat and steam for 10 minutes. Remove from the heat and carefully take out the cake pan. Set aside to cool for 10–12 minutes. Cut dhokla into 1-inch diamond shapes.
7. Heat oil in a small fry pan and add asafoetida and mustard seeds, covering with a lid to avoid splattering. Fry for a few seconds until mustard seeds stop popping. Remove from the heat, add curry leaves and cook for few seconds. Evenly spread the oil mixture over the dhokla pieces.
8. Transfer to a serving platter and garnish with fresh coriander and grated coconut.

Makes 6 servings
Serving size: ⅙ recipe
Amount per serving:

		Exchanges: 1½ starches	
		1 lean meat	
Calories	147	Carbohydrate	23 g
Fat	3.6 g	Dietary fiber	4.6 g
Saturated fat	0.5 g	Protein	5 g
Cholesterol	0 g	Sodium	376 mg

Poha

Pounded rice snack

This quick, simple dish is often served for breakfast, a snack or a light lunch.

2 cups poha (pounded rice)
¼ tsp turmeric
1 tsp salt
4 tsp vegetable oil
½ tsp mustard seeds
6–8 curry leaves
1 tbsp chana dal
1 small onion, thinly sliced
½ cup frozen peas
2 tsp coriander powder
½ tsp cayenne pepper (optional)
1 green chili, split lengthwise into two (optional)
⅓ cup water
1 tbsp fresh lemon juice
2 tbsp roasted Spanish peanuts (optional)

1. Clean poha and wash in 1–2 changes of cold water. Drain in strainer. Sprinkle with turmeric and salt and set aside.
2. Heat oil in a nonstick fry pan over medium high heat. Add mustard seeds and cover with a lid to avoid splattering. Fry for a few seconds until mustard seeds stop popping. Add curry leaves and chana dal. Cook until dal is light brown.
3. Add sliced onions and fry until light brown. Add peas, coriander powder, cayenne pepper and green chili. Stir, add water and bring to a boil. Reduce heat, cover and simmer for 7–8 minutes until peas are done.
4. Add poha and stir to mix well. Heat through and steam for about 2 minutes. Sprinkle with lemon juice and stir. Garnish with peanuts if desired.

Makes 6 servings (4 cups)
Serving size: ⅔ cup
Amount per serving:
Calories 178
Fat . . . . .5 g
Saturated fat . . . . 0.5 g
Cholesterol . . . . .0 g

Exchanges: 2 starches
1 fat

Carbohydrate . . . . 29 g
Dietary fiber . . . . .1.3 g
Protein . . . . 4 g
Sodium . . . . .370 mg

Uppama
Cream of wheat snack

Uppama is served most commonly at breakfast, although it may be served as a snack or a light meal. This is a very popular dish in south India. We enjoy it for lunch, so I usually put vegetables in it. It may also be made plain with just spices and/or onions.

1 cup cream of wheat
4 tsp vegetable oil
½ tsp mustard seeds
6–8 curry leaves
1 tbsp chana dal
1 small onion, thinly sliced
½ cup frozen peas
½ cup carrots, diced
½ tsp cayenne pepper (optional)
1 tsp salt
3½ cups water

1. Dry-roast cream of wheat in a heavy skillet, stirring constantly for 7–10 minutes until the cream of wheat turns light brown. Transfer to a plate and set aside.
2. Heat oil in the same skillet over medium high heat. Add mustard seeds, cover with a lid and fry for a few seconds until mustard seeds stop popping. Add curry leaves and chana dal. Cook until dal is light brown.
3. Add sliced onions and fry until light brown. Add peas, carrots, cayenne pepper and salt. Stir and fry for few seconds, add water and bring to a boil.
4. To the boiling water gradually add the roasted cream of wheat with one hand as you stir with the other. Keep stirring, breaking any lumps until the cream of wheat is well mixed with the water. Cover with a lid, reduce heat and simmer for 10–12 minutes until most of the water is absorbed.

5. Let stand until ready to serve. Stir before serving and garnish with fresh coriander if desired.

Makes 8 servings (4 cups)   *Exchanges: 1 starch*
Serving size: ½ cup   *1 vegetable*
                                                      ½ fat

Amount per serving:
Calories 115   Carbohydrate . . . . 19 g
Fat . . . . 2.7 g   Dietary fiber . . . . 2.3 g
Saturated fat . . . . 0.3 g   Protein . . . . 3 g
Cholesterol . . . . 0 g   Sodium . . . . 281 mg

Samosas
Potato-stuffed pastries

Samosas are one of the most-popular snacks of India. Potato-stuffed samosas are the most common, although they can be filled with lamb or something sweet. Hot samosas served with tea make any afternoon a delight. Serve them with coriander chutney, ketchup or tamarind chutney.

Filling
5 medium potatoes
2 tsp vegetable oil
½ tsp cumin seeds
1 tbsp chopped fresh ginger
¾ cup peas
2 tsp salt
1 tbsp coriander powder
1 green chili, chopped (optional)
1 tsp mango powder
1 tbsp garam masala
¼ cup water

Dough
2 cups flour
½ tsp salt
3 tbsp vegetable oil
½ cup water

Vegetable oil for frying

To prepare the filling:

1. Boil potatoes. To avoid potatoes from getting sticky, remove from boiling water as soon as they are done and cool completely.

2. Peel and mash boiled potatoes into small pieces (about ½-inch pieces), not necessarily of uniform size.

3. In a large fry pan, heat oil on medium high heat. When oil is hot, add cumin seeds. Fry for a few seconds until cumin seeds are golden brown, add ginger and stir. Add the mashed potatoes and the peas. Stir.

4. Add salt, coriander powder, green chili, mango powder and garam masala. Mix thoroughly. Add water. Cover with a lid, heat through, reduce heat to medium low and cook for 2–3 minutes. Stir and let stand covered for 5–7 minutes.

5. Open the lid and cool.

To prepare dough:

(This can be done in a food processor or dough maker.)

1. In a bowl, mix flour, salt and oil. Add water gradually as you mix.

2. Turn dough onto a floured surface and knead for 5 minutes or until dough becomes smooth and soft.

3. Divide dough into 10 balls.

To assemble samosas:

1. Roll each ball into a 5–6-inch circle. Cut in half. In a small bowl put about ¼ cup of water; set aside.

2. Take one half, dip your finger in water and run it along side the straight edge. Fold in half, joining the straight edges, making a cone. Seal edges tightly.

3. Fill with 2 tbsp of filling. Dip finger in water and run along the inside of the open mouth and seal tightly.

4. Keep filled samosas between dry towels to avoid drying.

5. Heat oil in a wok or fry pan over medium high heat. Oil is hot when you drop a pinch of dough into the oil and the dough floats up within seconds. (It is important to have the oil the right temperature because if the oil is too hot the samosas will not cook inside and if the oil is not hot enough the samosas might fall apart in the oil or get greasy.) Fry 3–5 samosas at a time until light golden brown, about 4–5 minutes on each side.

6. Serve hot with coriander chutney or ketchup. They can be reheated in the oven.

Makes 20 samosas   *Exchanges: 1 starch*
Serving size: 1 samosa   *1 fat*
Amount per serving:
Calories 125   Carbohydrate . . . . 16 g
Fat . . . . .6 g   Dietary fiber . . . . 1 g
Saturated fat . . . . 0.5 g   Protein . . . . 2 g
Cholesterol . . . . .0 g   Sodium . . . . .274 mg

My quick version

I love samosas but making them can be quite a task. I make my samosas with a tortilla for the shell. They taste great and take only quarter of the time and effort.

10 small flour tortillas*

2 tbsp flour

4 tbsp water

1. In a small bowl mix flour and water to make a paste; set aside.
2. Heat a frying pan over low heat.
3. Cut one tortilla into equal halves. Warm one of the halves in the frying pan for a few seconds. When it is soft, remove from pan. Immediately make into a cone using the flour paste instead of water to seal the edges. Follow the directions 2 to 6 above under To assemble samosas.

Makes 20 samosas   *Exchanges: 1 starch*
Serving size: 1 samosa   *1 fat*
Amount per serving:
Calories 114   Carbohydrate . . . . 16 g
Fat . . . . .5 g   Dietary fiber . . . . 1 g
Saturated fat . . . . 0.6 g   Protein . . . . 2 g
Cholesterol . . . . .0 g   Sodium . . . . .220 mg

---

* The fresher the tortillas, the easier it is to handle them. Homestyle tortillas do not work as well, however.

Indian breads

Wheat is the main staple food for north Indians. A variety of wheat breads are eaten at most meals. The most-common bread is roti or chapati. It is an unleavened bread made of whole wheat flour. The whole wheat flour available in India is made of a different variety of wheat that grinds up finer than the wheat flour available in the United States. Most stores that carry Indian groceries carry durum wheat flour or chapati flour, which comes from Canada. This flour makes softer Indian breads. If you are unable to get durum wheat flour, you can combine whole wheat flour with white flour to make the roties in the recipes.

The most-common roti is made on a tava (iron griddle). It is thin and flat, similar in appearance to a tortilla but very different in taste. For north Indians nothing is more satisfying and filling than a hot roti served with a meal. The varieties of breads include paratha plain or stuffed (pan fried), puri (deep fried) and kachori (stuffed puri).

Naan is a leavened flat bread made of white flour and is commonly served in restaurants. It is made in a clay oven, or tandoor, which gives this bread a very special taste.

Making roties is time-consuming and requires practice and skill. I have found making roties in the oven a great substitute and does not require the same skill or practice as making roties on a tava. I broil the roties and naan. Not every-one can have a tandoor in the house or go to the restaurant everyday, but everyone can enjoy the goodness of roti or naan at home. The taste of a warm roti is irresistible. Try these very simple, quick, low fat versions of Indian breads.

If durum wheat flour is not available, substitute ¾ cup whole wheat flour and ¼ cup white all-purpose flour for 1 cup of durum wheat flour. The amount of water needed to make the same consistency of dough for the two types of flours varies, so add water carefully.

For nutritional analysis, I used 3 parts whole wheat flour and 1 part white flour.

Tandoori roti
Oven chapati

Chapati, phulka and roti are all similar types of bread made of whole wheat flour. They look like tortillas but tastes quite different. They are typically made on a tava (iron griddle) on the stove top. Tandoori roti is supposed to be made in a tandoor (clay oven), but I make it in a conventional oven. This is a very easy and fast way to have roties with half the hassle.

2 cups durum wheat flour *or*
  1½ cups whole wheat flour and
  ½ cup all purpose flour
⅛–1 cup water
½ cup flour for rolling
2 tbsp ghee or butter (optional)

1. In a mixing bowl combine flours. (Dough can also be made in a food processor or dough maker.) Make a hole in the center of the flour. Add water gradually as you mix dough. (Depending on the type of flour, the amount of water needed may vary slightly.) The dough should be soft and easy to roll into a ball. Knead the dough thoroughly until smooth and elastic. Dough should resemble a bread dough in consistency and smoothness. Cover and let sit for 10 minutes or longer.
2. Preheat oven to broil.
3. Place ½ cup flour for rolling in a shallow container.
4. Divide dough into 8 balls. Roll each ball between the palms of your hands in a circular motion until the dough is smooth. Press to flatten. Roll each flat ball in the flour. Then roll each flat ball into approximately ¼-inch-thick oval or round flat breads.
5. Place 3–4 roties on a lightly greased baking sheet. Broil in the middle of the oven for 2–3 minutes (the roties will puff and become light brown). Turn over and broil for 1–2 minutes until slightly brown on the other side.

6. Serve immediately or place in air-tight container to serve later. Brush roti on the first side with ghee or butter, if desired.

Makes 8 roties   *Exchanges: 1½ starches*
Serving size: 1 roti
Amount per serving:
Calories 100   Carbohydrate . . . . 22 g
Fat . . . . .0 g   Dietary fiber . . . . 3 g
Saturated fat . . . . .0 g   Protein . . . . 4 g
Cholesterol . . . . .0 g   Sodium . . . . .0 mg

Phulka
Chapati

Phulka is typically a thin puffed whole-wheat bread. It is made on a tava (cast-iron flat griddle) on the stove top. If you do not have a tava use a heavy fry pan.

Roti dough (see recipe Tandoori roti on page 111)

1. Heat tava or a heavy fry pan on medium heat.
2. Place ½ cup flour for rolling in a shallow container.
3. Divide dough into 12 balls. Roll each ball between palms of your hands in a circular motion until the dough is smooth. Press to flatten. Roll each flat ball in the flour. Then using the flour as needed, roll into approximately 6-inch round flat breads.
4. Place the chapati on the heated tava or fry pan. The side that is facing the tava is the first side. Cook for a few (10-20) seconds until it turns color and becomes firm and easy to pick up, turn it over and cook on the other side. Cook until light brown on the second side, few (15-20) seconds. Turn it back to the first side and with a folded kitchen towel in one hand, press the chapati down gently but firmly. The chapati will puff as you press it.
5. Brush chapati on the first side with ghee or butter, if desired. Serve immediately or place in air-tight container to serve later.

Makes 12 phulkas
Serving size: 1 phulka
Amount per serving:

Exchanges: 1 starch

Calories	80	Carbohydrate	16 g
Fat	0 g	Dietary fiber	2 g
Saturated fat	0 g	Protein	3 g
Cholesterol	0 g	Sodium	0 mg

Tandoori alu roti

Potato-stuffed roti

A quicker and low fat version of potato paratha (pan fried), enjoy these as a satisfying meal with plain yogurt and salad.

Dough

2 cups durum wheat flour *or*
  1½ cups whole wheat flour and
  ½ cup all purpose flour
½ tsp salt
⅞–1 cup water
½ cup flour for rolling
2 tbsp ghee or butter

Filling

3 medium potatoes, boiled
½ tsp salt
½ tsp cayenne pepper (optional)
1 green chili, finely chopped, (optional)
1 tsp coriander powder

1. In a mixing bowl combine flour and salt. (Dough can be made in a food processor or dough maker.) Make a hole in the center of the flour. Add water gradually as you mix dough. (Depending on the type of flour, the amount of water needed may vary slightly.) The dough should be soft but easy to roll into a ball. Knead the dough thoroughly until smooth and elastic. Dough should resemble bread dough in consistency and smoothness. Cover and let stand for 10 minutes or longer.
2. Peel boiled potatoes. On a plate mash potatoes. The potatoes should be about ¼-inch pieces or smaller. Add salt, cayenne pepper, chopped green chili and coriander powder. Mix well. Divide filling into 12 equal portions.
3. Preheat oven on broil.

4. Place ½ cup flour for rolling in a shallow container.

5. Divide dough into 12 balls. Roll each ball with the palms of your hands in a circular motion until the dough is smooth. Press to flatten. Roll each flat ball in the flour. Roll out each ball into an approximately 3-inch circle. Place one portion of the filling in the center. Now lift all the edges of the circle, keeping the filling in the center, and join in the center. Crimp the edges tightly and flatten with the palm of your hand. Pick up the filled ball and roll again in the flour. Place the filled side down and roll to ¼-inch-thick oval or round flat breads.

6. Place 3–4 roties on lightly greased baking sheet. Broil in the middle of the oven. Broil for 2–3 minutes until light brown. Turn over and broil for another 1–2 minutes, until light brown on the other side.

7. Brush roti on the first side with ghee or butter. Serve immediately or place in an air-tight container to serve later.

Makes 12 roti
Serving size: 1 roti
Amount per serving:

Exchanges: 1½ starches

Calories	115	
Fat	2 g	
Saturated fat	1 g	
Cholesterol	5 g	

Carbohydrate	21 g
Dietary fiber	2.4 g
Protein	3 g
Sodium	199 mg

Ghee ke hath ki roti

Coiled roti

We all love this roti — it is crispy and has a very wheaty warm flavor. The name ghee (clarified butter) ke hath ki roti (roti made with ghee hands) may make you think it is high in fat, but it is not; it just uses ghee for rolling instead of flour. Cook roti until golden brown and crispy. Serve it with rajmah (kidney beans) or whole urd dal. You can also use margarine, if desired.

Roti dough (see recipe Tandoori roti on page 111)
2 tbsp ghee or butter

1. Heat tava (cast-iron flat griddle) or a heavy fry pan on medium heat.
2. Divide dough into 8 balls. Roll each ball between the palms of your hands until it is a smooth, flat ball. Lightly grease surface and rolling pin. Roll flat ball into an approximately ¼-inch-thick round, flat bread. Put ½ tsp ghee on the surface and spread with your finger. With the fingers lift one side and roll toward you, making it into a tight roll like a rope. Now take this roll and make a circle in a coiled shape. Pick it up in your palms, roll just a little bit and press so it will stick together into a flat circle. Roll again into a ¼-inch-thick flat bread, using a dab of ghee to help roll if necessary.
3. Place roti on the heated tava or fry pan. The side that is facing the tava is the first side. Cook for about 1 minutes. When the roti turns color or becomes firm and is easy to pick up, turn roti over and cook on the other side. Cook until light brown on the second side, about 1 minute. Remove and set aside or finish cooking as stated in the next step. I usually cook all the roties on the tava first and then place them under broiler.
4. Heat oven to broil. Place roties on a lightly greased baking sheet. Broil in the middle of the oven for 2–3 minutes until golden brown. Turn over and broil for another 1–2 minutes, until light brown.

. Brush roti on the first side with ½ tsp ghee. Serve immediately. This roti does not keep well. If you need to them cook in advance, cook on the tava and broil just before serving.

Makes 8 roties
Serving size: 1 roti
Amount per serving:
Calories 128
Fat . . . . .3 g
Saturated fat . . . . 1.8 g
Cholesterol . . . . .8 g

Exchanges: 1½ starches
½ fat

Carbohydrate . . . . 22 g
Dietary fiber . . . . 3 g
Protein . . . . 4 g
Sodium . . . . .1 mg

Missi roti

Chickpea flour roti

I grew up eating this roti for breakfast on Sunday mornings when the whole family was at home. This roti is very filling and tastes great. Of course it was extra filling growing up because mom served it with a scoop of fresh butter. We would dip it in creamy butter and eat it. But now I serve it with small amounts of butter and is not as heavy in the stomach.

2 cups durum wheat flour
1½ cup chickpea flour (besan)
1 medium onion, finely chopped
1 tsp salt
1⅛ cup water
½ cup wheat flour for rolling
2 tbsp butter

1. In a mixing bowl combine wheat flour, besan, chopped onions and salt; mix well. Add water gradually as you make the dough. The dough should be soft but easy to roll into a ball. Cover and set aside for 15 minutes. (This dough cannot be made in a food processor or dough maker as it tends to get sticky.)
2. Heat tava (cast-iron flat griddle) or a heavy fry pan on medium heat.
3. Place ½ cup flour for rolling in a shallow container.
4. Oil hands lightly and knead dough to make it smooth. Divide dough into 8 balls. Roll each ball between the palms of your hands until it is a smooth flat ball. Roll the ball in the flour. Then using the flour as needed, roll into approximately ¼-inch-thick round flat breads.
5. Place roti on the heated tava or fry pan. The side that is facing the tava is the first side. Cook for about 1 minutes until the roti turns color or becomes firm and is easy to pick up, turn it over and cook on the other side. Cook until light brown on the second side, about 1 minute. Remove and set aside or finish cooking as stated in the next step. Continue all roties in the same fashion.

6. Heat oven to broil. Place roties on a lightly greased baking sheet. Broil in the middle of the oven. Broil for 2–3 minutes until golden brown. Turn over and broil for another 1–2 minutes, until light brown.

7. Brush roti on the first side with ½ tsp butter. Serve immediately. This roti does not keep well. If you need to cook them in advance, cook on the tava and broil just before serving.

Makes 8 roties
Serving size: 1 roti
Amount per serving:
Calories 204
Fat .4 g
Saturated fat . . . . 1.8 g
Cholesterol . . . . .8 g

Exchanges: 2 starches
    1 fat

Carbohydrate . . . . 34 g
Dietary fiber . . . . .8.2 g
Protein . . . . 8 g
Sodium . . . . .311 mg

Naan

Pita bread

Naan originally came from the Middle East. It has become a very popular bread served in restaurants. It tastes much better than pita bread. It is supposed to be made in a tandoor (clay oven) but here is a way to make naans in your very own oven.

3 cups all-purpose flour
¾ cup nonfat plain yogurt
½ tsp active dry yeast
1 tsp sugar
½ cup lukewarm water
1 tbsp vegetable oil

1. In a food processor or dough maker combine flour and yogurt. (Dough can also be made by hand in a mixing bowl.)
2. Dissolve yeast and sugar in the lukewarm water. Add to flour and mix. Blend until dough is smooth. Dough should resemble bread dough in consistency and smoothness.
3. Transfer dough to a bowl, coat evenly with oil and knead a few times. Cover with a lid and let dough rise for 3–4 hours.
4. Divide dough into 12 equal portions. Roll between the palms of your hands to make smooth balls.
5. Preheat oven to broil.
6. Using lightly oiled surface and rolling pin, roll out each ball to about ¼-inch-thick oval shapes.
7. Place 3–4 naans on lightly greased baking sheet. Broil in the middle of the oven for 2–3 minutes until they are slightly puffed and become lightly browned. Turn over and broil for 1–2 minute. (Do not overcook the naans as they will become dry.)
8. Serve immediately or store in air-tight container.

Makes 12 naans
Serving size: 1 naan
Amount per serving:
Calories 124
Fat . . . . 1 g
Saturated fat . . . . 0 g
Cholesterol . . . . 0 g

Exchanges: 1½ starches

Carbohydrate . . . . 24 g
Dietary fiber . . . . 0.5 g
Protein . . . . 4 g
Sodium . . . . 11 mg

Paneer ke naan
Cheese-stuffed naan

Ricotta cheese or paneer can be used to make this very special recipe. My children love this bread.

Prepared naan dough (see recipe Naan on page 120)
1½ cup light ricotta cheese
½ tsp salt
1 tsp coriander powder
½ tsp cayenne pepper (optional)

1. Prepare naan dough; let rise.
2. In a heavy nonstick fry pan, add ricotta cheese and cook over medium heat, stirring occasionally. Cook until all the water is evaporated and the cheese is slightly crumbly. Transfer to a plate and cool completely. Add salt, coriander powder and cayenne pepper to the cheese and mix well.
3. Divide dough into 15 balls. Roll between the palms of your hands to make into smooth balls.
4. Using lightly oiled surface and rolling pin, roll out each ball to about 3-inch circle and place filling in the center. Lift the circle edges and bring to center, slightly overlapping, and crimp edges together. Press with the palm of your hand onto the rolling surface. Turn the stuffed ball over placing the filled side down. Cover and let sit for 5–10 minutes.
5. Preheat oven to broil.
6. Roll out each ball into ¼-inch-thick oval or circle shape, using oil if necessary.
7. Place naans on lightly greased baking sheet. Broil in the middle of oven. Broil for 2–3 minutes until they are lightly browned. Turn over and broil for another 1–2 minutes, until light brown.
8. Serve immediately or store in air-tight container.

Makes 15 naans
Serving size: 1 naan
Amount per serving:
Calories 133
Fat . . . . 3 g
Saturated fat . . . . 1 g
Cholesterol . . . . 8 g

Exchanges: 1 starch
1 lean meat

Carbohydrate . . . . 20 g
Dietary fiber . . . . 0.6 g
Protein . . . . 6 g
Sodium . . . . 111 mg

Rice

Rice is the staple in south and east India. Rice is the most-versatile grain available. Rice *can be cooked plain or with meat, vegetables and a variety of spices. In India mostly plain rice is eaten. Plain rice goes well with dal, meat, vegetable or yogurt.*

Long grain and basmati rice are the most-common kinds of rice eaten in India. Basmati rice is an extra long grain rice with a naturally mild aroma. The basmati rice is a little more expensive and often eaten on special occasions or for special rice dishes like pulao *or* biriyani. *When cooked, basmati rice is long, slender and fluffy. Long grain rice is a little more sticky and has a very good taste. Parboiled or other packaged rice are generally not used in Indian meals.*

Rice is easy to cook if you keep a few easy steps in mind. In my cooking classes, people often mention how difficult it is to cook fluffy rice. Here are some general rules to help cook perfect rice.

1. Use a pan large enough for the rice to expand. My general rule of thumb is 1 quart pan for every cup of rice, for example, one quart for 1 cup, 2 quarts for 2 cups. You can use a larger pan but if you use a smaller one you will have sticky rice or unevenly cooked rice as the rice will get packed and not have room to expand. Make sure the pan has a tightly fitted lid.

2. If you buy packaged long grain rice you do not have to clean it. If you buy basmati rice, you might have to clean it of any extraneous materials like small rocks or unhulled rice. Always wash rice in 3–4 changes of water. Washing gets rid of any starchy powder and makes the rice less sticky. To wash rice, place it in a bowl and add cold water. I usually stir with my hand as I lightly rub the rice. Place your hands at the end of the bowl as you drain the water. Repeat the process until the water is relatively clear.

3. Soak the rice for about 30 minutes. Soaking rice makes the rice grains longer and reduces the stickiness.

4. Drain rice and discard the water.

5. Add 2 cups of water for 1 cup of rice. For each additional cup of rice, reduce the water by ¼ cup; for example, for 2 cups of rice use 3¾ cups of water, for 3 cups of rice use 5½ cups of water.

6. Bring the rice a to full boil, reduce the heat and simmer uncovered for about 7 minutes. Partially cover with lid and continue to simmer undisturbed for another 7–8 minutes. Check if the rice is done by placing 1 or 2 grains of rice on the counter top and gently pressing with a finger. If the rice is not done, you will feel the grain under your finger. If the rice is done, remove it from the heat, cover with a lid and let stand until ready to serve.

7. Before serving, gently fluff rice with a fork or a butter knife. Lift rice and gently break up the any lumps.

8. To reheat rice, steam with a tablespoon of water. If available, use a microwave oven.

Basmati chawal
Plain rice

Basmati rice is a variety of rice that is extra long and has a very nice aroma. When cooked it is fluffy and light. Some people eat basmati rice everyday and some people use it only for special occasions or special rice dishes. It cooks just like other rice.

1 cup basmati rice
2 cups water

1. Clean rice, removing any unhulled rice or other extraneous material. Wash in 2–3 changes of water until washing water is relatively clear. Soak in cold water for ½ hour or longer. (Soaking helps to make the rice grains longer. If you don't have time, this soaking can be eliminated.) Drain the rice in a strainer.
2. Add rice and 2 cups of water in a 2-quart or larger saucepan. Bring water to a boil. Reduce heat to a simmer. Cover with a lid, leaving a small crack open for steam to escape. Simmer for 10–15 minutes. All the water should be absorbed. Check if rice is done by placing 1 or 2 grains of rice on the counter top and gently pressing with your finger. If the rice is not done you will feel the grain under your finger.
3. Remove from the heat. Cover with a lid until ready to serve. Before serving, stir gently from the bottom with a fork as you fluff the rice.

Makes 10 servings (3½ cups)   *Exchange: 1 starch*
Serving size: ⅓ cup
Amount per serving:

Calories 68	Carbohydrate . . . . 15 g
Fat . . . . .0 g	Dietary fiber. . . . . .0.2 g
Saturated fat . . . . .0 g	Protein . . . . 1 g
Cholesterol . . . . .0 g	Sodium . . . . .0 mg

Neembu chawal
Lemon rice

In south India this is a very popular side dish. It is great for leftover rice.

1 cup long grain rice, cooked (see recipe Basmati chawal on page 128)
1 tbsp vegetable oil
½ tsp mustard seeds
6–8 curry leaves
1 tbsp chana dal
⅛ tsp turmeric
½ tsp cayenne pepper (optional)
2 tbsp fresh lemon juice
1 tsp salt

1. Cook rice and cool slightly.
2. Heat oil in heavy skillet over medium high heat. Add mustard seeds and cover with a lid to avoid splattering until mustard seeds stop popping. Add curry leaves and chana dal. Cook for a few seconds until dal is light brown. Remove from heat. Stir in turmeric and cayenne pepper. A few seconds later add lemon juice.
3. Add rice and salt, mixing gently to avoid breaking rice. Return to the stove and heat through.
4. Serve cold or warm.

Makes 10 servings (3½ cups)   *Exchange: 1 starch*
Serving size: ⅓ cup
Amount per serving:

Calories	77	Carbohydrate	15 g
Fat	1 g	Dietary fiber	0.2 g
Saturated fat	0 g	Protein	1 g
Cholesterol	0 g	Sodium	214 mg

Bhuna chawal

Roasted rice

This rice tastes and smells great. The whole spices add wonderful flavor to the rice. Yet the flavor is not overpowering and is an excellent accompaniment to any party. The whole spices, by the way, are not eaten

1½ cups basmati rice

¼ tsp cumin seeds

6–8 black peppercorns

½-inch cinnamon stick

2 cloves

1 whole cardamom, crushed

2 bay leaves

2 tsp vegetable oil

3 cups water

1 tsp salt

1. Clean rice, removing any unhulled rice or other extraneous material. Wash in 2–3 changes of water until the water is relatively clear. Soak in cold water for ½ hour or longer. (Soaking can be eliminated for time sake).

2. Drain the rice in a strainer; set aside.

3. Combine cumin seeds, peppercorn, cinnamon stick, cloves, cardamom and bay leaves in a small bowl; set aside.

4. Heat oil in a 2–3 quart saucepan over medium high heat. Add the spices and fry for a few seconds until the cumin seeds are golden brown. (All the spices will puff.) Add drained rice and fry for 2–3 minutes, stirring constantly. Take care not to break the rice.

5. Add 3 cups of water and salt. Bring to a boil and reduce heat to a simmer. Partially cover with a lid, leaving a small crack open for steam to escape. Simmer for 15–20 minutes. All water should be absorbed. Check if rice is done by placing 1 or 2 grains of rice on the counter top and gently

pressing with your finger. If the rice is not done you will feel the grain under your finger.

6. Remove from the heat. Cover with a lid until ready to serve. Before serving, fluff rice with a fork by gently stirring from the bottom.

Makes 15 servings (5 cups)
Serving size: ⅓ cup
Amount per serving:

Calories 73	Carbohydrate . . . . 15 g
Fat . . . . 0.5 g	Dietary fiber . . . . 0.2 g
Saturated fat . . . . 0 g	Protein . . . . 1 g
Cholesterol . . . . 0 g	Sodium . . . . 143 mg

Exchange: 1 starch

Matar pulao
Rice pilaf with peas

This is a great addition to a special meal. In my house it was often served with coriander chutney and plain yogurt as a quick and light Sunday lunch. This low fat version has all the flavor of the traditional pulao with a fraction of the fat.

1½ cups basmati rice
½ tsp cumin seeds
2 cloves
½-inch stick cinnamon
2 cardamom pods
2 bay leaves
1 tbsp vegetable oil
1 small onion, thinly sliced
¾ cup peas
1½ tsp garam masala
2¾ cups water
1 tsp salt

1. Clean rice, removing any unhulled rice or other extraneous material. Wash in 2–3 changes of water until washing water is relatively clear. Soak in cold water for ½ hour or longer.
2. Drain the rice in a strainer; set aside.
3. Combine the whole spices, cumin seeds, cinnamon stick, cloves, cardamom and bay leaves in a small bowl; set aside.
4. Heat oil in a 3–4 quart saucepan over medium high heat. Add the whole spices and fry for a few seconds until the cumin seeds are golden brown. (All the spices will puff.) Add the sliced onions and fry until onions are golden brown. Add the strained rice and fry for 2–3 minutes longer, stirring constantly. Take care not to break the rice.
5. Add peas, garam masala, 2¾ cups of water and salt. Stir gently to mix.

6. Bring to a boil and reduce heat to a simmer. Partially cover with a lid, leaving a small crack open for steam to escape. Simmer for 15–20 minutes, gently stirring once or twice. All water should be absorbed. Check if rice is done by placing 1 or 2 grains of rice on the counter top and gently pressing with your finger. If the rice is not done, you will feel the grain under your finger.
7. Remove from the heat. Cover with a lid until ready to serve. Before serving, gently stir and fluff rice with a fork by gently stirring from the bottom.

Makes 8 servings (6 cups)   *Exchanges: 2 starches*
Serving size: ¾ cup   *½ fat*
Amount per serving:

Calories	169	Carbohydrate	30 g
Fat	3.5 g	Dietary fiber	1 g
Saturated fat	0.5 g	Protein	3 g
Cholesterol	0 g	Sodium	281 mg

Tahari

Vegetable rice

Tahari can be made with the vegetables of your choice. It is often made with cauliflower and potatoes or peas. I use mixed vegetables for convenience and variety. Serve with plain yogurt and coriander chutney or pickles for a light, quick meal.

1 cup long grain or basmati rice
2½ cups water
1 tsp salt
1 cup frozen mixed vegetables
1 tsp vegetable oil
½ tsp cumin seeds
¼ tsp turmeric
¼ tsp garam masala
1 tsp lemon juice

1. Clean rice, removing any unhulled rice or other extraneous material. Wash in 2–3 changes of water until water is relatively clear. Soak in cold water for ½ hour or longer. (Soaking helps to make the rice grains longer. If you don't have time, this soaking can be eliminated). Drain the rice in a strainer.

2. Add rice, 2 cups of water and ¾ tsp salt in a 2-quart saucepan. Bring water to a boil. Reduce heat to simmer. Cover with a lid, leaving a small crack open for steam to escape. Simmer for 10–15 minutes. All the water should be absorbed. Check if rice is done by placing 1 or 2 grains of rice on the counter top and gently pressing with your finger. If the rice is not done you will feel the grain under your finger.

3. In the meantime heat vegetable oil in a heavy 2–3 quart saucepan over medium heat. Add cumin seeds and fry for a few seconds until cumin seeds are golden brown. Add the frozen mixed vegetables, ¼ tsp salt, turmeric and ½ cup water. Bring to a boil, cover with a lid, reduce heat and simmer for 10 minutes. Add garam masala and stir.

4. Add rice to the vegetables, mixing gently to avoid breaking rice. Sprinkle with lemon juice and stir. Cover and let sit until ready to serve.

Makes 8 servings (4 cups)　　*Exchanges: 1½ starches*
Serving size: ½ cup
Amount per serving:
Calories . . . . 100　　Carbohydrate . . . . 21 g
Fat . . . . 0.5 g　　Dietary fiber . . . . 0.7 g
Saturated fat . . . . 0 g　　Protein . . . . 2 g
Cholesterol . . . . 0 g　　Sodium . . . . 274 mg

Subji biriyani
Vegetable-rice casserole

Biriyani is most commonly made with lamb or chicken. This one has all the goodness of vegetables and beans and tastes great—a meal in itself.

1 cup basmati rice
½ cup moong dal
5 cups water
¼ tsp turmeric
1½ tsp salt
¼ cup unsalted dry roasted peanuts
1 small onion
½ tsp cumin seeds
1 tsp cayenne pepper (optional)
2 tbsp oil
1 small potato, peeled and chopped into ¼-inch cubes
1 medium carrot, peeled and chopped into ¼-inch cubes
1 small tomato, chopped into ½-inch cubes
½ cup frozen peas
¼ cup cashews, chopped
¼ cup golden raisins
½ cup nonfat plain yogurt

1. Clean rice and moong dal of any extraneous material. Combine them and wash in 2 to 3 changes of water until washing water is relatively clear. Strain and set aside.
2. In a 2–3 quart sauce pan, add the rice and dal mixture, 3 cups of water, turmeric and 1 tsp salt. Bring to a boil. Reduce heat to a simmer. Cover with a lid, leaving a small crack open for steam to escape. Simmer for 12–15 minutes until all the water is absorbed and the rice is done.
3. In the meantime, coarsely grind peanuts in a blender and set aside.

4. To make the onion masala, in the same blender jar finely grind onions, cumin seeds and cayenne pepper. (You may need to add 1–2 tbsp water to be able to grind.) Set aside.
5. Heat a heavy nonstick 4-quart skillet, add ground onions. Cook for a few minutes until most of the water is evaporated. Add oil and fry until onion masala is light brown.
6. Add ground peanuts, chopped potatoes, carrots, tomatoes, peas, cashews, raisins and 1 tsp salt. Mix well. Add 1 cup water, bring to a boil and reduce heat. Cover with a lid and simmer until vegetables are tender, about 8–10 minutes, stirring occasionally.
7. Whip yogurt lightly and add 1 tbsp at a time to the vegetables, stirring constantly. Cook for 5–7 minutes without covering, stirring occasionally to blend the yogurt with the vegetables.
8. Add the remaining 1 cup water and bring to a boil.
9. Add the cooked rice and dal. Stir gently with spatula to avoid breaking rice. Cover with a lid and steam through for 2–3 minutes.
10. Remove from the heat, close the lid and let stand until ready to serve. Fluff with a fork before serving.

Makes 6 servings (6 cups)   *Exchanges: 3 starches*
Serving size: 1 cup   *2 fats*
Amount per serving:
Calories 310   Carbohydrate . . . . 45 g
Fat . . . . 10 g   Dietary fiber . . . . 3 g
Saturated fat . . . . 1.5 g   Protein . . . . 9 g
Cholesterol . . . . 0 g   Sodium . . . . .573 mg

Meethe chawal
Sweet rice

Sweet rice is usually served at the end of a meal. Here is an easy, low fat and foolproof method of making this dish.

1 cup basmati rice
2 cups water
¼ tsp saffron threads
½-inch cinnamon stick
1 cup sugar
2 tbsp blanched slivered almonds

1. Clean rice, removing any unhulled rice or other extraneous material. Wash in 2 to 3 changes of water until washing water is relatively clear. Soak in cold water for ½ hour or longer. (Soaking helps to make the rice grains longer. If you don't have time, this soaking can be eliminated.) Drain the rice in a strainer.
2. In a 2-quart saucepan add water, saffron threads and cinnamon stick. Bring water to a boil, add rice and bring to a boil again. Reduce heat to a simmer. Cover with a lid, leaving a small crack open for steam to escape. Simmer for 15–20 minutes. All water should be absorbed. Check if rice is done by placing 1 or 2 grains of rice on the counter top and gently pressing with your finger. If the rice is not done, you will feel the grain under your finger.
3. Add sugar, cover with a lid and cook for 1–2 minutes. Remove from the heat and let sit for about 10–15 minutes. Open the lid and mix gently with a fork. Cover and let sit for 10 minutes or until ready to serve.
4. Before serving, fluff rice with a fork by stirring gently from the bottom. Garnish with almonds.

Makes 12 servings (4 cups)
Serving size: ⅓ cup
Amount per serving:
Calories 123
Fat . . . . 0.5 g
Saturated fat . . . . 0 g
Cholesterol . . . . 0 g

Exchanges: 2 starches

Carbohydrate . . . . 29 g
Dietary fiber . . . . 0.3 g
Protein . . . . 1 g
Sodium . . . . 0 mg

Idli

Steamed rice dumplings

Idlies are originally from south India, but now they have become very popular all over India. This is an easy recipe and the idlies comes out very light and fluffy. Serve them with sambhar and coconut chutney.

½ cup urd dal
1¼ cup cream of rice
1 cup water
1 tsp salt

1. Clean dal of any extraneous materials and soak for 2 hours or longer.
2. Wash soaked dal in 3–4 changes of water until water is relatively clear. Drain dal in a strainer. Place dal and ⅔ cup water into a blender jar. Grind to a fine paste.
3. In a large bowl add cream of rice and ⅓ cup of cold water. Mix well. Add the dal paste to the cream of rice. Add salt and stir thoroughly.
4. Cover with a lid. Keep in a warm place for 20–24 hours. The dough will ferment and almost double in size. (I usually ferment it overnight and steam it the next night for dinner.)
5. Stir the fermented mixture very gently to mix the top and bottom, using a folding motion.
6. Brush or spray idli containers with oil. Fill idli containers to the top line of the indentation, about ¼ cup each. Place 1 cup water to a boil in a pan that holds the idli container. Once water is boiling, place the filled idli container and cover with a lid. Reduce heat and steam for 10 minutes. Remove the idli container and cool slightly. Using a butter knife remove idlies and place in a container lined with a towel. Wrap with towel. (Idlies can be steamed in a cake pan by placing them, about 1 inch deep and steaming as above.)
7. Serve warm with sambhar and coconut chutney.

Makes 24 idlies
Serving size: 2 idlies
Amount per serving:

Exchange: *1 starch*

Calories 94
Fat . . . . 0 g
Saturated fat . . . . 0 g
Cholesterol . . . . 0 g

Carbohydrate . . . . 19 g
Dietary fiber . . . . 2.4 g
Protein . . . . 3 g
Sodium . . . . 181 mg

Murgh biriyani
Chicken-rice casserole

This is a very popular dish made on special occasions. Here is a much lower fat version of the biriyani. Served with salad and coriander chutney—it makes a great meal.

1½ cups basmati rice
1 lb skinless, boneless chicken
2 tbsp vegetable oil
½ tsp cumin seeds
4 cardamom pods
8 black peppercorns
4 cloves
1-inch stick cinnamon
2 bay leaves
1 medium onion, fined sliced
2 garlic cloves, crushed
¼ tsp turmeric
1 tsp ginger, finely chopped
1 cup plain nonfat yogurt
2 tsp salt
3½ cups water

1. Clean rice removing any unhulled rice or other extraneous material. Wash in 2–3 changes of water until washing water is relatively clear. Soak in cold water for ½ hour or longer. (Soaking helps to make the rice grains longer. If you don't have time, this soaking can be eliminated.) Drain the rice in a strainer.
2. Cut chicken into bite-size pieces. (I usually have the butcher do this.) Wash and drain thoroughly. Dry with paper towel. Set aside.
3. Heat oil in a heavy skillet over medium high heat. Add cumin seeds, cardamom pods, black peppercorns, cloves, cinnamon stick and bay leaves. Fry for a few seconds until cumin seeds are golden brown. Add sliced onion, garlic and ginger. Fry until onions are soft and transparent.

4. Add chicken pieces and fry for 3–4 minutes or until chicken turns white and firm, stirring frequently. Add turmeric and stir to mix.
5. Whip yogurt with a fork. Add to chicken gradually 1–2 tbsp at a time, stirring constantly. Cook on high heat until most of the liquid is evaporated and yogurt masala clings to the chicken. Add salt and water. Bring to a boil, cover with a lid and reduce heat and simmer for 5–7 minutes.
6. Add rice, bring to a boil, reduce heat and cover with a lid. Simmer for 15–17 minutes until rice is done.
7. Let stand covered until ready to serve.

Makes 8 servings (8 cups)
Serving size: 1 cup
Amount per serving:
Calories 241
Fat . . . . 5.0 g
Saturated fat . . . . 1 g
Cholesterol . . . . 32 g

Exchanges: 2 starches
1½ lean meat

Carbohydrate . . . . 31 g
Dietary fiber . . . . 0.7 g
Protein . . . . 16 g
Sodium . . . . 584 mg

Kheechri
Rice and bean porridge

Kheechri is a light meal often served like a porridge. Moong dal is considered to be the easiest pulse to digest. It tastes great served with pickles, roasted papad and plain yogurt. This kheechri is best when slightly overcooked. You can still see the rice and dal grain but it is well blended (porridge-like consistency).

1 cup long grain rice
¾ cup split moong
2 tsp ghee
pinch of heeng (asafoetida)
½ tsp cumin seeds
½ tsp turmeric
1½ tsp salt
5 cups water

1. Clean rice and moong dal of any extraneous material. Combine them and wash in 2–3 changes of water, until water is relatively clear. Strain and set aside.
2. Heat the ghee in heavy skillet over medium high heat. Add asafoetida and cumin seeds and cook for a few seconds until cumin seeds are golden brown. Add the strained rice, moong dal, turmeric, salt and water. Bring to a boil. Reduce heat and partially cover with a lid, leaving a slight crack open to avoid boiling over. Simmer for 30–35 minutes, stirring occasionally. Serve hot.

Makes 12 servings (6 cups)
Serving size: ½ cup
Amount per serving:
Calories 106
Fat .1 g
Saturated fat . . . . .0 g
Cholesterol . . . . .0 g

Exchanges: 1 starches
1 lean meat

Carbohydrate . . . . 20 g
Dietary fiber . . . . .1.2 g
Protein . . . . 4 g
Sodium . . . . .269 mg

Beans, legumes and pulses

Dal is technically a dried, dehusked, split bean. But the word dal in India is used loosely for all pulses (legumes) and beans. The pulses are used in all their different forms. They are used as a whole bean, split with husk, split without husk and polished (commonly known as washed) or ground as flour. Most of the dals are available in stores that carry Indian groceries. Local supermarkets also have some dals but usually only the whole variety, for example, chickpeas, brown lentils or kidney beans.

Dals are used extensively in the Indian diet. For vegetarians, dals provide the essential protein. For centuries Indians have combined dal and rice or chapati (bread) for the main course. Dal is often the "entree" so to speak. A vegetarian meal is often planned around what goes best with the particular dal, similar to a nonvegetarian meal being planned around what goes best with the particular meat.

Dals are very versatile. Most have a mild but distinct taste and texture. The variety of things made with dals in India is unlimited and includes main courses, snacks and desserts.

Some of the most-common dals used in India are listed below.

Chana dal (bengal gram): This is the split, polished variety of the bengal gram bean. This looks like the yellow split peas but it is smaller in size and sweeter in flavor. It is used in many recipes other than as a soup or dal. For example, it is used as a seasoning in many south Indian dishes. It is also ground to make a flour known as besan. The whole bean (kala chana) looks similar to chickpeas but is smaller in size, has a black husk and has a different taste.

Chickpeas (garbanzo beans or kabuli chana): I prefer to use the dried chickpeas. I will sometimes use the canned chickpeas for convenience.

Chickpea flour: See Besan under spices section.

Kidney beans (rajmah): I usually use the dried red kidney beans. On occasion I will substitute canned ones for convenience.

Black-eyed peas (lobhia): They are also known as cowpeas. Use dried or canned varieties for convenience.

Lentils (masoor): They are used whole or split and polished. The whole masoor (sabut masoor) is sold as lentils in the United States. The polished, split variety (dhuli masoor) is salmon colored and may be sold as red split lentils.

Moong beans (green gram): Moong dal is sold whole, split with skin or dehusked and polished. Each type of moong dal has a distinct taste, so use the one your recipe calls for.

Toor dal (pigeon peas or arhar dal): Toor dal is sold split and polished only. It comes from a red gram whole bean, but the whole variety is rarely used. Toor dal is sold as regular or oily type. I prefer the regular one but you can wash the oily one in hot water to remove the oil.

Urd dal (black gram): This dal is sold whole, as split with skin or split and polished. Each type has a distinct use in a recipe, so notice which one the recipe calls for.

Cooking dals takes time, especially whole dals. Most Indians use pressure cookers for cooking dals. Pressure cookers save significant amounts of cooking time. I have included the amount of time needed to cook dals using the pressure cooker. If you have never used a pressure cooker, see pressure cooker instructions under Time-saving tips.

Soaking also cuts down on cooking time, but dals can

be cooked without soaking. Soaking especially helps with whole beans like kidney beans or chickpeas (garbanzo beans). The split and dehusked varieties take the least amount of time to cook.

In the United States, people associate beans with bloating and stomach discomfort. This discourages them from using beans in their diet. In India beans have been a staple for centuries. The use of spices and seasonings reduces the discomfort associated with beans and dals by aiding the digestive process. Asafetida, turmeric, ginger, onions and garlic all improve the digestibility of beans.

If you are not used to eating beans, start with a small serving and increase it gradually as you build tolerance.

Exchanges are calculated based on the carbohydrate and protein content. The calories may be less than the computed exchanges as the beans are high in protein and carbohydrate.

Sukha lobhia
Black-eyed peas

My quick version of black-eyed peas uses canned peas. It is great as a snack or a side dish.

(16 oz) can black-eyed peas (dried black-eyed peas can be
used, soaked and cooked until tender)
tsp oil
pinch of asafetida
tsp cumin seeds
tsp turmeric
tsp cayenne pepper (optional)
tsp coriander powder
tsp salt
cup water
tsp garam masala
tsp lemon juice

In a strainer drain and rinse canned black-eyed peas. Set aside.
In a heavy nonstick skillet heat oil over moderate heat. In hot oil add
asafetida and cumin seeds. Cook for few seconds until cumin seeds are
golden brown. Add drained black-eyed peas and stir. Add turmeric,
cayenne pepper, coriander powder, salt and water. Stir to mix.
Bring to a boil. Cover with a lid and reduce heat. Simmer for 10–12
minutes. Most of the water should be absorbed.
Add garam masala and lemon juice. Stir. Transfer to a serving platter.

Makes 4 servings (2 cups)		*Exchanges: 1 starch*
Serving size: ½ cup		*1 lean meat*
Amount per serving:		
Calories 88		Carbohydrate . . . . 13 g
Fat . . . . 1.5 g		Dietary fiber . . . . 5 g
Saturated fat . . . . .0 g		Protein . . . . 6 g
Cholesterol . . . . .0 g		Sodium . . . . .270 mg

Toor da

Pigeon peas

Toor dal is the most-versatile dal. This plain version is nice because it is easy and can be served with any spicy vegetable. It has a mild flavor that combines with other side dishes without clashing flavors.

1 cup toor dal

4 cups water

1 tsp salt

¼ tsp turmeric

1 tsp vegetable oil

a pinch of asafetida

¼ tsp cumin seeds

1 tsp coriander powder

1 tbsp fresh coriander, finely chopped (optional)

1. Clean toor dal of any extraneous materials. Wash dal in 2–3 changes of water.

2. In a heavy skillet add toor dal, 4 cups of water, salt and turmeric. Bring to a boil on medium high heat. Reduce heat, cover with a lid and simmer for 30–40 minutes. The dal will be tender and soupy. (The dal and water should not separate.) To cook in a *pressure cooker* put cleaned dal, 3 cups of water, salt and turmeric in the pressure cooker. Cover with a lid and put the pressure weight in place. Cook on medium high heat until pressure develops, reduce heat and cook under pressure for 5 minutes. Cool the cooker to remove pressure. Open the lid carefully. Return to the stove and continue to simmer until the dal is of desired consistency as stated above.

3. To prepare the chounk (seasoning): In a small fry pan heat oil to a near smoking point. Add asafetida and cumin seeds and cook for a few seconds until cumin seeds are golden brown. Remove from the heat and add coriander powder. Immediately add chounk to the dal. Stir.

. Transfer to a serving platter, garnish with chopped coriander if desired. Serve hot. Dal thickens as it cools.

Makes 8 servings (4 cups)   *Exchanges: 1 starch*
Serving size: ½ cup   *½ lean meat*
Amount per serving:
Calories 90   Carbohydrate . . . . 15 g
Fat . . . . 1 g   Dietary fiber . . . . 3 g
Saturated fat . . . . 0 g   Protein . . . . 5 g
Cholesterol . . . . 0 g   Sodium . . . . .271 mg

Sprouted moong

This is very popular way to prepare moong or moth dal as it is called in my husband's home (Rajasthan). It needs a little planning as it takes two to three days to soak and sprout the dal. I have at times sprouted enough for two to three meals and frozen the sprouted dal. Once sprouted it cooks very fast. My children love this served over rice with a little ghee and sugar sprinkled on top (of course that is how my husband eats it too).

1 cup whole moong

1 tsp vegetable oil

A pinch of asafetida

½ tsp cumin seeds

¼ tsp turmeric

1 tsp coriander

¼ tsp cayenne pepper (optional)

¾ tsp salt

¾ cup water

1. Clean moong of any extraneous materials. Wash in 2–3 changes of water. Cover with water and soak overnight.
2. Drain the water from soaked moong. Wrap drained moong in a cloth (old kitchen towel or a large handkerchief works well) and place in a bowl. Pour ½ cup water over the cloth to keep the moong and cloth moist and cover with a lid. Keep in a warm place like the oven for 24–36 hours. (To speed the process I sometimes turn on the oven light.) The moong should have little sprouts (¼-inch or so).
3. Place sprouted moong in a colander and rinse in fresh water.
4. Heat oil in a heavy pan over medium high heat. When the oil is hot, add a pinch of asafetida and the cumin seeds. Fry for a few seconds until golden brown.
5. Add sprouted moong, turmeric, coriander powder, cayenne pepper (optional), salt and ¾ cup water. Stir. Bring to a boil. Cover and reduce

heat and simmer for 20–30 minutes. Check moong for tenderness. It is done when soft to the touch but still firm.

5. Open the lid, increase heat and evaporate any excess water accumulated at the bottom. Transfer to a serving bowl.

Makes 6 servings (3 cups)   *Exchanges: 1 starch*
Serving size: ½ cup   *1 lean meat*
Amount per serving:

Calories	122	Carbohydrate	20 g
Fat	1 g	Dietary fiber	2.7 g
Saturated fat	0 g	Protein	8 g
Cholesterol	0 g	Sodium	272 mg

Masoor dal
Lentil soup

To get the best flavor of this dal, cook until the water and dal do not separate. Serve it over rice or with any good bread.

1 cup lentils (whole masoor)
6 cups water
1 tsp salt
½ tsp turmeric
1 tsp vegetable oil
a pinch of asafetida
½ tsp cumin seeds
1 tsp fresh lemon juice

1. Clean masoor dal of any extraneous material. Wash in 2–3 changes of water.
2. In a medium saucepan combine masoor dal, 6 cups of water, salt and turmeric. Bring to a boil on high heat. Reduce heat, cover tightly with a lid and simmer for about 1½ hours, until the lentils are very soft. To cook in a *pressure cooker* put the lentils, 4 cups of water, salt and turmeric in pressure cooker. Cover with a lid and put pressure weight in place. Cook on medium heat until pressure develops, reduce heat and cook under pressure for 20 minutes. Cool completely before opening pressure cooker. Return to stove and continue to simmer.
3. Check for desired consistency. For best results cook lentils until the beans and water do not separate.
4. To prepare chounk (seasoning): In a small fry pan, heat oil to a near smoking point then add asafetida and cumin seeds. Fry for a few seconds until cumin seeds are golden brown. Add the chounk to the dal.
5. Add lemon juice and stir. Transfer to a serving bowl.

Makes 8 servings (4 cups)
Serving size: ½ cup
Amount per serving:

Calories 90
Fat . . . . 0.8 g
Saturated fat . . . . 0 g
Cholesterol . . . . 0 g

Exchanges: 1 starch
       1 lean meat

Carbohydrate . . . . 14 g
Dietary fiber . . . . 4.5 g
Protein . . . . 7 g
Sodium . . . . 269 mg

Dal makhani

Whole urd dal

This is the dal most-commonly served in restaurants in the United States. In restaurants the chefs cook it with cream to give it a very smooth, rich taste. I never use cream and find the longer you cook it, the creamier and mellower the taste becomes.

¾ cup whole urd dal
2 tbsp dried black-eyed peas (lobhia)
9 cups water
1 tsp salt
½ tsp turmeric
1 tbsp fresh ginger, chopped
4 tsp vegetable oil
a pinch of asafoetida
½ tsp cumin seeds
1 cup onion, thinly sliced
2 tsp coriander powder
½ tsp cayenne pepper (optional)

1. Clean urd dal and black-eyed peas of any extraneous materials. Wash in 2–3 changes of water.
2. Add beans and 9 cups of water, salt, turmeric and ginger in a heavy 4-quart saucepan and bring to a boil on high heat. Reduce heat and simmer for 3–3½ hours until dals are done and the water and beans do not separate. The long cooking time gives it a reddish brown color and the creamy taste. Add more water if it becomes too thick, depending on how much water is evaporated during simmering. To cook in a *pressure cooker* add drained dals and 6 cups of water, salt, turmeric and ginger. Cover with a lid and put pressure weight in place. Cook on medium high heat until the pressure develops. Reduce heat and cook under pressure for 45 minutes. Cool the cooker until pressure is removed. Open the lid

carefully. Stir, checking for consistency as above. If the dal is not well blended, return to heat and cook under pressure again for 10–15 minutes.

3. To prepare onion masala heat oil in a nonstick fry pan on medium high heat. Add asafetida and cumin seeds and cook for a few seconds until cumin seeds are golden brown. Add sliced onions. Stir constantly, frying until onions are golden brown. Remove from the heat. Add coriander and cayenne pepper. Add the onion masala to the boiled beans and simmer for 5–7 minutes.

4. Transfer to a serving platter and serve hot.

Makes 8 servings (4 cups)   *Exchanges: 1 starch*
Serving size: ½ cup   *1 lean meat*
Amount per serving:

Calories 97	Carbohydrate . . . . 14 g
Fat . . . . 2.5 g	Dietary fiber . . . . 6 g
Saturated fat . . . . 0 g	Protein . . . . 5 g
Cholesterol . . . . 0 g	Sodium . . . . 272 mg

Rajmah
Kidney beans

Rajmah is a specialty of the state of Punjab. Kidney beans take a long time to cook but now with the pressure cooker the time is reduced drastically. When in a hurry, use drained and rinsed canned kidney beans. Substitute 2 cans for 1 cup of dry beans. Serve rajmah with rice or roti.

1 cup kidney beans
6 cups water
1 tsp salt
¼ tsp turmeric
1 medium tomato
1 medium onion
1 tbsp fresh ginger, chopped
½ tsp cumin seeds
2 tbsp vegetable oil
⅓ cup plain nonfat yogurt
2 tsp coriander powder
½ tsp cayenne pepper (optional)
½ tsp garam masala
2 tbsp fresh coriander leaves, chopped (cilantro)

1. Clean kidney beans and remove any extraneous materials. Wash in 2–3 changes of water. Soak overnight in 4 cups of water.
2. In a heavy saucepan, pour in the kidney beans and its soaking water plus 2 cups of fresh water and salt. Cook on high heat, bringing the water to a boil. Reduce heat, cover with a lid and simmer for about 2 hours or until beans are very tender. The kidney beans should be slightly split and mash easily with a spoon against the side of the pan. To cook in a *pressure cooker* pour in the kidney beans with its soaking water and salt. Do not add the additional 2 cups of water. Cover with a lid and put the pressure weight in place. Once pressure develops, reduce heat and cook under pressure for 20 minutes. Cool the cooker until the pressure is removed.

Open the lid carefully. Check beans for tenderness. The kidney beans should be as soft as stated above.

3. In the meantime grind tomato, onion, ginger and cumin seeds to a smooth paste. Set aside.

4. In a nonstick frying pan add ground onion paste. Cook over medium high heat, stirring occasionally until all the water evaporates. Add the oil and continue frying until the onion masala is light brown.

5. Lightly whip yogurt and add 1 tbsp at a time to the onion masala as you continue to fry. Add coriander and cayenne pepper. Stirring constantly, continue to fry the mixture until most of the liquid in the pan evaporates and the mixture is thick enough to draw away from the sides and bottom of the pan in a dense mass.

6. Add the mixture to the boiled beans and stir thoroughly. Bring to a boil and reduce heat to a simmer for 10 minutes. Stir in garam masala and 1 tbsp of chopped coriander. Remove from the heat.

7. Transfer to a serving dish and garnish with the remaining fresh coriander.

Makes 8 servings (4 cups)
Serving size: ½ cup
Amount per serving:
Calories 125
Fat . . . . 3.5 g
Saturated fat . . . . 0 g
Cholesterol . . . . 0 g

Exchanges: 1 starch
1 lean meat

Carbohydrate . . . . 17 g
Dietary fiber . . . . 7.4 g
Protein . . . . 6 g
Sodium . . . . 278 mg

Chana dal aur lauki
Chana dal with celery

Traditionally this dal is cooked with lauki (bottle gourd). In the summer I do use lauki, often available in specialty stores. Celery, however, makes a nice substitute and is available all year.

1 cup chana dal
1 cup celery, diced
6 cups water
1 tsp salt
½ tsp turmeric
1 tsp vegetable oil
a pinch of asafetida
¼ tsp cumin seeds
2 tsp lemon juice to taste

1. Clean the chana dal of any extraneous materials. Wash chana dal in 3–4 changes of water. Set aside.
2. Clean celery, pull the threads and discard. Chop celery into ½-inch pieces. Set aside.
3. In a medium saucepan add chana dal, 6 cups of water, salt and turmeric. Bring to a boil on medium high heat. Reduce heat, cover with a lid leaving a slight crack open and simmer for 1–1½ hours until the lentils are very soft and turning soupy. Stir with an egg beater or a wire wisk 2–3 times to blend dal into the water. The dal and water should not separate. To cook in *pressure cooker* put chana dal, 4 cups of water, salt and turmeric in a pressure cooker, cover with a lid and put pressure weight in place. Cook on medium high heat until pressure develops. Reduce heat and cook under pressure for 15 minutes. Cool until pressure is removed. Open the lid carefully. Check for desired consistency and whisk as mentioned above. Return to the stove.
4. Add chopped celery and simmer for 10–12 minutes until celery is tender.

4. To prepare chounk (seasoning): In a small fry pan, heat oil to near smoking point. Add asafetida and cumin seeds and cook for a few seconds until cumin seeds are golden brown. Add chounk to the dal.
5. Remove from the heat, add lemon juice and stir. Transfer to a serving dish.

Makes 8 servings (4 cups)   *Exchanges: 1 starch*
Serving size: ½ cup   *1 lean meat*
Amount per serving:
Calories 100   Carbohydrate . . . . 15 g
Fat . . . . 2 g   Dietary fiber . . . . 7 g
Saturated fat . . . . 0 g   Protein . . . . 5 g
Cholesterol . . . . 0 g   Sodium . . . . 298 mg

Sukhi moong dal

Dry moong dal

This dal is cooked until just tender and served dry instead of soupy like most dals. It goes great with roti or rice. Sometimes my mother would serve it as an after-school snack.

1 cup dehusked moong dal (yellow)
1½ cups water
¼ tsp turmeric
1 tsp salt
2 tsp vegetable oil
pinch of asafetida
¼ tsp cumin seeds
½ tsp cayenne pepper (optional)
2 tsp coriander powder
½ tsp garam masala
2 tsp lemon juice

1. Clean moong dal of any extraneous materials. Wash in 3–4 changes of water.
2. In a medium saucepan add moong dal, water, turmeric and salt. Bring to a boil. Reduce heat, cover with a lid and simmer for 12–15 minutes. Do not overcook the dal. (The dal should be tender to touch but intact.) Remove from the heat and set aside.
3. To prepare chounk (seasoning): Heat oil in a large nonstick fry pan over medium heat. Add asafetida and cumin seeds and cook for a few seconds until cumin seeds are golden brown. Add the cooked dal to the chounk. Add cayenne pepper, coriander powder, garam masala and lemon juice. Stir carefully with a spatula to avoid mashing or breaking the dal. Cook for 5–7 minutes, stirring occasionally, allowing any liquid that has accumulated to evaporate.
4. Transfer to a serving platter and garnish with fresh coriander if desired.

Makes 6 servings (about 3 cups)
Serving size: ½ cup
Amount per serving:

Calories	123	Carbohydrate	20 g
Fat	1 g	Dietary fiber	1.7 g
Saturated fat	0 g	Protein	8 g
Cholesterol	0 g	Sodium	364 mg

Exchanges: 1 starch
1 lean meat

Gujrati dal
Sweet-and-sour dal

This is a sweet-and-sour toor dal, a specialty of the state of Gujarat. It tastes great with rice or as a soup.

¾ cup toor dal
4 cups water
1 tsp salt
¼ tsp turmeric
1 large tomato
4 tsp sugar
1 tbsp lemon juice
1 tsp vegetable oil
a pinch of asafetida
¼ tsp mustard seeds
4–6 curry leaves
1 tbsp chopped fresh coriander (optional)

1. Clean toor dal of any extraneous materials. Wash in 3–4 changes of water.
2. In a saucepan add toor dal, water, salt, turmeric and the whole tomato. Bring to a boil on high heat. Reduce heat, cover with a lid and simmer for 45–60 minutes until the dal is tender and soupy. (The dal and water should not separate.) Continue to simmer on low heat as you go through the next steps. To cook in a *pressure cooker* put cleaned dal, 3 cups of water, salt, turmeric and the whole tomato in a pressure cooker. Cover with a lid and put pressure weight in place. Cook on medium heat until pressure develops. Reduce heat and cook under pressure for 5 minutes. Cool until pressure is removed. Open the lid carefully. Return to stove and continue to simmer. Check for consistency as above.
3. Take out the tomato and pass it through a sieve. Add the tomato juice to the dal and stir. Discard the seeds and skin. Lightly wisk the dal with wire wisk or egg beater, 2–3 whisks only, to blend the dal.

4. Add sugar and lemon juice. Stir.
5. To prepare chounk (seasoning): Heat oil in a small fry pan over medium high heat. Add asafetida and mustard seeds, cover with a lid to avoid splattering and fry for a few seconds until mustard seeds stop popping. Remove from the heat, add curry leaves and fry for a few seconds. Add the chounk to the dal. Stir.
6. Transfer to a serving platter, garnish with fresh coriander and serve hot.

Makes 8 servings (4 cups)   *Exchange: 1 starch*
Serving size: ½ cup
Amount per serving:

Calories 80	Carbohydrate . . . . 14 g
Fat .1 g	Dietary fiber . . . . .2.5 g
Saturated fat . . . . .0 g	Protein . . . . 4 g
Cholesterol . . . . .0 g	Sodium . . . . .271 mg

Kaddi

Chickpea soup

Kaddi is a very popular dish throughout northern India. It is prepared in various ways but this is the most-common version in my home. It is often made with sour yogurt. It can be prepared with fresh yogurt using lemon juice to add the sour taste. Serve it with rice.

1½ cups plain nonfat yogurt*
1½ cups besan (chickpea flour), sifted
5⅓ cups water
½ tsp turmeric
½ tsp cayenne pepper (optional)
1½ tsp salt
2 tsp vegetable oil
pinch of asafetida
¼ tsp fenugreek seeds
¼ tsp cumin seeds
2 dried whole red chilies
oil for frying
2 tsp lemon juice†

1. Mix yogurt, ¾ cup besan, 5 cups water, turmeric, cayenne pepper and 1 tsp salt. Set aside.
2. In a large heavy skillet, heat oil to near smoking point add asafetida, fenugreek seeds, cumin seeds and whole red chilies. Cook for a few seconds until cumin seeds are golden brown. Add yogurt mixture and stir. Cook on medium high heat. Bring to a boil, stirring frequently. The

---

* For best results use sour yogurt that has sat out overnight.

† Adjust lemon juice based on how sour the yogurt is. The amount listed (2 tsp) is based on fresh yogurt.

mixture may boil over, so be careful and stir as needed. Once the mixture has come to a full boil, reduce heat, partially cover with a lid and simmer for 30 minutes, stirring occasionally.

3. In the meantime mix ¾ cup besan and ⅓ cup of water. Whip with hand or electric mixer until light and fluffy. To test the mixture, get a cup of cold water and drop a small amount of blended besan paste in the water. The paste should float to the top. If it does not, continue to beat with mixer and repeat process. When the paste floats to the top, add ½ tsp of salt. Set aside.

4. In a medium fry pan or wok, heat the oil (about 1 inch deep) on high heat. When the oil is very hot, make pakories (besan balls), using a teaspoon or fingertips to add about 1 tsp of besan paste at a time to the oil. Add as many balls as the fry pan will hold in a single layer. Fry on one side until light brown, turn over and fry the other side. Drain onto a paper towel. Repeat process until all the besan paste is used.

5. In a medium bowl add about 2 cups of very hot water. Add the pakories and soak for 10–20 minutes.

6. Drain the pakories and add them to the kaddi. Simmer for 5 minutes. Add lemon juice and stir.

7. Transfer to a serving bowl. Serve with lemon on the side to accommodate individual tastes.

Makes 9 servings (6 cups) *Exchanges: 1 milk*
Serving size: ¾ cup *1 fat*
Amount per serving:

Calories	117	Carbohydrate	13 g
Fat	5 g	Dietary fiber	4.3 g
Saturated fat	0.5 g	Protein	5.6 g
Cholesterol	0 g	Sodium	397 mg

Sambhar
Toor dal with vegetables

There are as many ways to cook sambhar as there are cooks. This is a very popular way to cook dal throughout southern India. Serve with idli or rice.

1 cup toor dal
6 cups water
1½ tsp salt
½ tsp turmeric
1 medium onion, chopped into ½-inch cubes
1 medium tomato, chopped into 1-inch cubes
½ cup carrots, sliced
½ cup green beans, chopped
3 tbsp sambhar powder (see recipe page 54)
1 tsp tamarind paste
2 tsp vegetable oil
a pinch of asafetida
½ tsp mustard seeds
6–8 curry leaves

1. Clean toor dal of any extraneous materials. Wash in 2–3 changes of water.

2. In a heavy saucepan add toor dal, 6 cups of water, salt and turmeric. Bring to a boil on high heat. Reduce heat, cover with a lid and simmer for 45–50 minutes until the dal is tender and soupy. (The dal and water should not separate.) Keep dal simmering on low heat as you go through the next remaining steps. To cook in a *pressure cooker* put cleaned dal, 4 cups of water, salt and turmeric in the cooker. Cover with a lid and put pressure weight in place. Cook on medium heat until pressure develops, reduce heat and cook under pressure for 5 minutes. Cool until the pressure is removed. Open the lid carefully. Return to the stove and continue to simmer. Check for consistency as above.

3. In the meantime, chop the vegetables. When the dal is well done, add the onions, tomatoes, carrots, green beans and sambhar powder. Bring to a boil, reduce heat and simmer for about 10 minutes until vegetables are done.
4. Add the tamarind paste and continue to simmer.
5. To prepare chounk (seasoning): Heat oil in a small fry pan. Add asafetida and mustard seeds, cover with a lid to avoid splattering and cook for a few seconds until mustard seeds stop popping. Remove from the heat, add curry leaves and cook for few seconds. Add the chounk to the dal mixture and stir.
6. Transfer to a serving bowl and serve hot.

Makes 10 servings (5 cups)
Serving size: ½ cups
Amount per serving:
Calories 86
Fat . . . . 1 g
Saturated fat . . . . 0 g
Cholesterol . . . . 0 g

Exchanges: 1 starch
1 lean meat

Carbohydrate . . . . 15 g
Dietary fiber . . . . 3.2 g
Protein . . . . 5 g
Sodium . . . . 327 mg

Chole

Spicy chickpeas

Chole is becoming a very popular dish all over India. It originates from the state of Punjab and in north India it is available at most restaurants. Many street vendors carry chole with puri or bhatura (fried breads). People eat them as a meal or a snack. It is usually served hot but is also great cold for picnics. The most-popular version is made in a tamarind sauce and is fairly spicy (not necessarily chili hot). For best results use dry chickpeas and cook them until they are very soft. The flavor of chole improves as the spices blend with the chickpeas. I usually cook chole three to four hours before I want to serve them.

1½ cups dried chickpeas (garbanzo beans)
6 cups water
1½ tsp salt
2×1 inch dried tamarind *or* 1 tsp tamarind concentrate pulp
½ cup boiling water
4 tsp oil
½ tsp cumin seeds
2 cloves
2 bay leaves
1-inch cinnamon stick
1 cup onions, thinly sliced
2 garlic cloves (optional)
1 tsp fresh ginger, chopped
½ cup tomatoes, chopped
1 tbsp coriander powder
1½ tsp garam masala
½ tsp cayenne pepper (optional)
1 small green chili, chopped (optional)
2 tbsp fresh coriander, finely chopped (cilantro)

1. Clean chickpeas and remove any extraneous materials. Wash chickpeas in 2–3 changes of water. Soak overnight in 4 cups of water.
2. In a heavy saucepan, add the chickpeas and its soaking water plus 2 cups of fresh water and salt. Cook on high heat, bringing the water to a boil. As white froth develops, skim with a large slotted spoon and discard. Reduce heat, cover with a lid and simmer for about 2 hours or until beans are very tender. The chickpeas should be slightly split and mash easily with a spoon against the side of the pan. As you stir the chickpeas some of them will fall apart, (that is how soft you want them). To cook in a *pressure cooker* pour in the chickpeas with its soaking water and salt. (Do not add the additional 2 cups of water.) Boil on high heat. Skim the white froth and discard. Cover with a lid and put the pressure weight in place. Once pressure develops, reduce heat and cook under pressure for 30 minutes. Cool the cooker until all the pressure is removed. Open the lid carefully. Check beans for tenderness. The chickpeas should be as soft as stated above.
3. In the meantime soak the dried tamarind in ½ cup boiling water. Let stand for 20 minutes or longer. Squeeze the tamarind with your fingers and thumb. Squeeze and strain all the juice and discard the extraneous material as you will only use the tamarind juice. Set aside. If you are using the tamarind paste, mix in boiling water and set aside.
4. Heat oil in a nonstick fry pan over medium high heat. Add cumin seeds, cloves, bay leaves and cinnamon stick. Fry for a few seconds until cumin seeds are golden brown. Add onions, garlic and ginger and cook until onions are golden brown, stirring frequently. Reduce heat, adding the chopped tomatoes. Cook for 2–5 minutes until tomatoes are tender, stirring frequently.
5. Add the onion masala (spice mixture), coriander powder, garam masala, cayenne pepper and the green chili to the boiled chickpeas. Add the tamarind juice and stir thoroughly. Bring to a boil and reduce heat. Cover and simmer for 30 minutes, stirring occasionally.
6. Transfer to a serving platter. Garnish with fresh chopped coriander before serving.

Makes 8 servings (4 cups)
Serving size: ½ cup
Amount per serving:
Calories 161
Fat . . . . .4 g
Saturated fat . . . . .0 g
Cholesterol . . . . .0 g

Exchanges: 1 starch
1 medium fat meat
Carbohydrate . . . . 24 g
Dietary fiber . . . . .11.6 g
Protein . . . . 7 g
Sodium . . . . .415 mg

Vegetables

Indians generally love vegetables. Because of the tropical climate, the variety of vegetables available in India is much more extensive than in the colder climate of the Western World. Large numbers of Indians are vegetarians so they have created unlimited ways of preparing vegetables. Vegetables are never just boiled; spices are used to add flavor and variety.

The vegetables are either cooked dry (sukhi subji) or in a sauce (tari subji). The preparation of vegetables varies from state to state and from household to household. Some recipes may call for cooking them just enough to make it tender while others may require them to be simmered until the vegetables are soft and well blended with the spices.

When in a hurry I often use frozen vegetables. I am also likely to use my food processor to grate or chop vegetables if possible. I rarely use canned vegetables except tomato sauce or chopped tomatoes. Even in a hurry I use all the spices the dish calls for. The way I see it, whether you use one spice or six it takes the same amount of time. The spices are what adds the flavor, variety and taste.

Vegetables are usually cooked in a fair amount of oil, either fried or roasted with spices. I have found the amount of oil needed to bring out the flavor and taste can be drastically reduced. Over the years I have successfully reduced the amount of oil used in dishes without compromising the taste therefore, a minimum amount of oil is used to roast or fry the spices. Use a nonstick pan for the dry vegetables (sukhi subji). Although the prepared vegetables are not fat free, the amount of fat is very low.

If you thought vegetables are boring, hold on and give your palate a real treat!

Jeera alu
Spicy new potatoes

My mother made these with small new potatoes fresh out of the garden. I use the canned potatoes as they are convenient and always available. If you choose to use fresh new potatoes, steam them and follow the directions.

2 (16 oz) cans whole new potatoes
2 tbsp vegetable oil
½ tsp cumin seeds
¼ tsp turmeric
1 tsp salt
1 tbsp coriander powder
¼ tsp cayenne pepper (optional)
½ tsp mango powder
1 tsp garam masala

1. Drain and rinse canned potatoes. Cut any potatoes larger than 1 inch into half.
2. Heat oil in a heavy fry pan or a wok on medium heat. When oil is hot, add cumin seeds and cook for a few seconds until seeds turn golden brown. Add drained potatoes and stir.
3. Add the remaining spices and stir.
4. Reduce heat and fry for 15 to 20 minutes, stirring occasionally. Transfer to a serving platter.

Makes 6 servings (3 cups)
Serving size: ½ cup
Amount per serving:
Calories 95
Fat . . . . .5 g
Saturated fat . . . . 0.5 g
Cholesterol . . . . .0 g

Exchanges: 1 starch
1 fat
Carbohydrate . . . . 13 g
Dietary fiber . . . . .2.3 g
Protein . . . . 1 g
Sodium . . . . .350 mg

Gobhi gajar ki subji
Cauliflower mixed vegetables

This is one of my family's favorite vegetable. It is colorful and has a nice blend of flavors. Cauliflower is typically fried or cooked in a fair amount of oil, but I add the oil at the end, to bring a similar flavor with a fraction of the fat.

1 small cauliflower (3 cups), divided into small florets (1-inch)
1½ cups carrots, peeled and thinly sliced (¼-inch)
1½ cups zucchini, thinly sliced (¼-inch)
4 tsp vegetable oil
a pinch of asafetida
½ tsp cumin seeds
1 tsp fresh ginger, chopped
¼ tsp turmeric
1½ tsp salt
½ tsp cayenne pepper (optional)
1 tbsp coriander powder
½ tsp mango powder
¾ tsp garam masala
1 tbsp fresh coriander, finely chopped (cilantro)

1. Wash and drain cauliflower, carrots and zucchini. Set aside.
2. Heat 1 tsp oil in a heavy, nonstick skillet over medium high heat. Add asafetida and cumin seeds and cook for a few seconds until seeds are golden brown.
3. Add vegetables and stir. Add ginger, turmeric, salt and cayenne pepper. Stir thoroughly.
4. Heat through, cover with a lid and reduce heat. Simmer for 8–10 minutes. Open 1–2 times to stir the vegetables. Cook until vegetables are tender but firm.

5. Sprinkle with coriander powder, mango powder and garam masala. Stir carefully in a lifting and turning fashion so as not to mash the vegetables.

6. Add the remaining 3 teaspoons of oil around the sides of the pan, allowing the oil to get to the bottom of the pan. All the liquid from the vegetables should be evaporated; if not, increase heat to evaporate it. Fry for 3–5 minutes, stirring once or twice in the same lifting and turning fashion. (This final roasting or frying in the oil brings out the true flavor of this dish.)

7. Transfer to a serving platter. Garnish with fresh coriander.

Makes 8 servings (4 cups)	*Exchanges: 1 vegetable*
Serving size: ½ cup	*½ fat*
Amount per serving:	
Calories 40	Carbohydrate . . . . 5 g
Fat . . . . 2.5 g	Dietary fiber . . . . 1.7 g
Saturated fat . . . . 0 g	Protein . . . . 1 g
Cholesterol . . . . 0 g	Sodium . . . . 282 mg

Alu matar

Potato and pea curry

This vegetable goes with anything. It is a favorite of children and adults alike. I use tomato sauce for convenience. Substitute one medium tomato, juiced, if desired.

3 medium potatoes
1 tsp oil
¼ tsp cumin seeds
¾ cup peas, frozen or fresh
½ cup tomato sauce or 1 large tomato, ground
½ tsp turmeric
2 tsp coriander powder
¼ tsp cayenne pepper (optional)
¾ tsp salt
2½ cups water
½ tsp garam masala
1 tbsp chopped fresh coriander (cilantro)

1. Peel and wash potatoes. Cut into 1½-inch pieces. Set aside.
2. Heat oil in a heavy saucepan over medium heat. Add cumin seeds and cook for a few seconds until the seeds are golden brown.
3. Add washed and drained potatoes, peas and tomato sauce. Stir.
4. Add turmeric, coriander powder and cayenne pepper. Stirring constantly, cook until the tomato sauce is dry and coats the potatoes.
5. Add water and salt. Bring to a boil. Reduce heat, cover with a lid and simmer for 15–20 minutes. The potatoes should be tender and the curry (gravy) should be slightly thick.
6. Add the garam masala. Transfer to a serving dish and garnish with fresh coriander.

Makes 6 servings (3 cups)   *Exchange: 1 starch*
Serving size: ½ cup
Amount per serving:
Calories 90   Carbohydrate . . . . 19 g
Fat .1 g   Dietary fiber . . . . 2 g
Saturated fat . . . . .0 g   Protein . . . . 2 g
Cholesterol . . . . .0 g   Sodium . . . . .410 mg

Bharva hari mirch
Stuffed bell peppers

To make any meal look and taste special, serve this very colorful and elegant dish.

4 small bell peppers
4 tsp vegetable oil
¼ tsp mustard seeds
4 cups shredded cabbage
½ cup grated carrots
⅛ tsp turmeric
1 tsp salt
1 tsp coriander powder
¼ tsp cayenne pepper (optional)

1. Wash and dry the bell peppers. Cut the bell peppers lengthwise (from the stem side) in half. Remove the seeds and cut out the pulp part near the stem, leaving the pepper in a cup-like form. Set aside.
2. Heat 1 tsp of oil in a large, nonstick fry pan over medium heat. Add mustard seeds, covering with a lid to avoid splattering. Fry for a few seconds until the mustard seeds stop popping. Add the shredded cabbage and carrots. Stir.
3. Add turmeric, salt, coriander powder and cayenne pepper and stir. Cover with a lid, heat through, reduce heat and simmer for 5–7 minutes. The vegetables should be slightly tender. If there is any excess liquid accumulated at the bottom of the pan, increase heat to evaporate it. Remove from the heat and cool to room temperature.
4. Divide cabbage mixture into eight equal parts. Stuff the bell pepper halves with the mixture.
5. Clean the fry pan and heat the remaining 3 tsp of oil over medium heat. Place the stuffed bell peppers in the hot oil with the stuffed side facing up.

. Reduce heat, cover with a lid and simmer for 10–12 minutes until the bell peppers become tender. The bottom of the bell peppers will be slightly black. Transfer the bell peppers to a serving tray.

Makes 8 servings   *Exchange: 1 vegetable*
Serving size: ½ pepper
Amount per serving:

Calories 40	Carbohydrate . . . . 5 g
Fat . . . . .2 g	Dietary fiber . . . . .1.6 g
Saturated fat . . . . .0 g	Protein . . . . 1 g
Cholesterol . . . . .0 g	Sodium . . . . .275 mg

Gajar ki subji
Sweet-and-sour carrots

We love this carrot dish. It tastes a little like glazed carrots, but much more flavorful. This is how it was made at my grandmother's house.

1 lb carrots
1 tsp vegetable oil
¼ tsp cumin seeds
⅛ tsp fenugreek seeds
¼ tsp turmeric
½ tsp salt
2 tsp coriander powder
¼ tsp cayenne pepper (optional)
¼ cup water
½ tsp mango powder
1 tbsp sugar

1. Peel and washed carrots. Slice into thin (¼-inch) circles. (I often slice carrots in the food processor.) Set aside.
2. Heat oil in a heavy skillet over medium high heat. Add cumin and fenugreek seeds and fry for a few seconds until seeds are golden brown.
3. Add carrots and stir. Add turmeric, salt, coriander powder, cayenne pepper and water. Stir, cover with a lid, reduce heat and simmer for 10–12 minutes. Carrots should be tender to the touch.
4. Add mango powder and sugar. Stir. Cook for 3–5 minutes. All the liquid from the carrots should be evaporated. If not, increase heat to evaporate it. Transfer to a serving dish.

Makes 5 servings (2½ cups)   *Exchanges: 2 vegetables*
Serving size: ½ cup
Amount per serving:
Calories 45   Carbohydrate . . . . 9 g
Fat . . . . .1 g   Dietary fiber . . . . 2 g
Saturated fat . . . . .0 g   Protein . . . . 1 g
Cholesterol . . . . .0 g   Sodium . . . . .255 mg

Palak alu

Spinach and potatoes

*For this recipe I usually use frozen spinach for convenience; although
 me stores carry washed spinach in the salad area. Try it for an extra
 ecial taste.*

10-oz package of frozen chopped spinach
medium potato
tsp vegetable oil
½ tsp cumin seeds
½ tsp salt
½ tsp turmeric
tsp coriander powder
½ tsp cayenne pepper (optional)

. Thaw frozen spinach. Set aside. Peel, wash and cut potato into 1-inch
pieces. Set aside.

. Heat oil in a nonstick skillet over medium heat. Add cumin seeds and fry
for a few seconds until cumin seeds are golden brown.

. Add potatoes and spinach and sprinkle with salt, turmeric, coriander
powder and cayenne pepper. Stir to mix.

. Cover with a lid and heat through. Reduce heat and simmer for 12–15
minutes until potatoes are tender to the touch. Stir once or twice.

. If their is any excess liquid accumulated, increase heat to evaporate it.
Transfer to a serving dish.

Makes 4 servings (2 cups)　　　*Exchanges: 2 vegetables*
Serving size: ½ cup
Amount per serving:

Calories 55	Carbohydrate . . . . 10 g
Fat . . . . .1 g	Dietary fiber. . . . . .1.7 g
Saturated fat . . . . .0 g	Protein . . . . 2 g
Cholesterol . . . . .0 g	Sodium . . . . .321 mg

Kaddu

Sweet-and-sour winter squash

In my house this dish was made during festivals and served with puri or kachori (fried breads). Kaddu cooked in this style is my personal favorite vegetable. In India we always used the pumpkin to make this recipe, but a good cooking pumpkin is not always available here. So I find butternut squash is an excellent substitution. The fenugreek seeds give this recipe a unique flavor.

1 small butternut squash (2 lb)*
2 tsp vegetable oil
¼ tsp cumin seeds
⅛ tsp fenugreek seeds
½ tsp turmeric
¾ tsp salt
2 tsp coriander powder
½ tsp cayenne pepper (optional)
⅓ cup water
1 tbsp lemon juice
2 tbsp sugar

1. Peel and cut butternut squash in half. Scoop out and discard the inside seeds and threads. Cut into about 1-inch pieces. Rinse, drain and set aside.
2. In a frying pan heat oil on medium high heat. Add cumin and fenugreek seeds and cook for a few seconds until seeds are golden brown.
3. Add the chopped squash, turmeric, salt, coriander powder, cayenne pepper and water. Stir to mix. Cover with a lid and bring to a boil.

---

* Most squash are very hard to cut. If you have a microwave, heat the whole squash on high for 1–2 minutes until just warm—an amazingly easy way to peel and cut it.

Reduce heat and simmer for 15–18 minutes until the squash is soft to the touch. Stir occasionally.

4. Add lemon juice and sugar. Mash the squash with a potato masher or large spoon. Simmer for 5–7 minutes. Transfer to a serving dish.

Makes 4 servings (2 cups)   *Exchange: 1 starch*
Serving size: ½ cup
Amount per serving:

Calories 80	Carbohydrate . . . . 17 g
Fat . . . . 2 g	Dietary fiber . . . . 1.8 g
Saturated fat . . . . 0 g	Protein . . . . 1 g
Cholesterol . . . . 0 g	Sodium . . . . 403 mg

Bund gobhi
Cabbage and peas

Here is a quick and simple way to cook cabbage. Cabbage can be cooked by itself or with potatoes or peas (as in this recipe). If cooked to the right tenderness (tender but not overcooked), the sweet flavor of cabbage comes through.

1 medium head cabbage (about 2 lb)
2 tsp vegetable oil
½ tsp mustard seeds
½ cup frozen peas
¼ tsp turmeric
¾ tsp salt
2 tsp coriander powder
¼ tsp cayenne pepper (optional)

1. Remove any tough or discolored cabbage leaves and discard. Cut cabbage into four. Remove core and thinly slice the cabbage into ¼-inch strips. Set aside.
2. Heat oil in a heavy skillet or wok over medium heat. When oil is hot add mustard seeds, cover with a lid to avoid splattering and cook for a few seconds until the seeds stop popping.
3. Add sliced cabbage and the frozen peas. Stir.
4. Add turmeric, salt, coriander powder and cayenne pepper. Stir to coat the spices. Cover with a lid and heat through. Reduce heat and simmer for 6–8 minutes until the cabbage becomes transparent and slightly tender.
5. Remove lid, increase heat and cook for another 3–5 minutes to evaporate any juices that may have accumulated. Stir occasionally. Transfer to a serving dish.

Makes 8 servings (4 cups)
Serving size: ½ cup
Amount per serving:

Calories 30	Carbohydrate . . . . 4 g
Fat . . . . 1 g	Dietary fiber . . . . 1.5 g
Saturated fat . . . . 0 g	Protein . . . . 1 g
Cholesterol . . . . 0 g	Sodium . . . . .218 mg

Exchange: 1 vegetable

Bhindi tamatar ki subji
Okra with tomatoes

Okra is a very popular vegetable in India. It is usually cooked as a dry vegetable. Pick only the tender okra because tough okra does not cook well or absorb any of the spices. I usually add fennel seed powder in my okra recipes to bring out the unique flavor of this vegetable.

1 lb fresh tender okra *or* frozen whole okra
4 tsp vegetable oil
½ tsp cumin seeds
1 medium onion, thinly sliced
1 medium tomato, cut in half and sliced into ¼-inch wedges
½ tsp turmeric
1 tsp salt
1 tbsp coriander powder
½ tsp cayenne pepper (optional)
2 tsp fennel seeds, coarsely ground
½ tsp mango powder

1. Wash and drain okra leaving no water in the okra. Remove the top end and the bottom tip. Slice okra in half. Set aside. (If using frozen okra, thaw and slice.)
2. Heat 1 tsp of oil in a nonstick fry pan over medium high heat. Add cumin seeds and fry for a few seconds until seeds turn golden brown.
3. Add sliced onions and tomatoes and layer sliced okra on top. Sprinkle turmeric, salt, coriander powder, cayenne pepper and ground fennel seeds. Stir gently with spatula using a lifting and turning motion.
4. Cover with a lid, reduce heat and simmer for 8–10 minutes. Okra should be tender to the touch.
5. Remove lid, increasing heat to medium. Add mango powder and stir gently as mentioned above. Pour the remaining 3 tsp oil around the sides

of the pan, allowing oil to get to the bottom of the pan. Fry for 5–7 minutes, stir once or twice in the same lifting and turning fashion.
5. Transfer to a serving platter.

Makes 6 servings (3 cups)   *Exchanges: 1 vegetable*
Serving size: ½ cup   *½ fat*
Amount per serving:
Calories 55   Carbohydrate . . . . 6 g
Fat .3 g   Dietary fiber . . . . .1.3 g
Saturated fat . . . . 0.4 g   Protein . . . . 1 g
Cholesterol . . . . .0 g   Sodium . . . . .360 mg

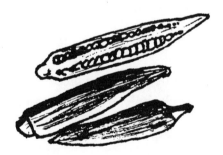

Alu gobhi

Potatoes with cauliflower

The potato is called the king of vegetables in India. Potatoes are often added to many meat, vegetable and rice dishes. Alu gobhi is a wonderful combination and it tastes great hot or cold.

1 medium cauliflower (4 cups)
2 medium potatoes
4 tsp vegetable oil
½ tsp cumin seeds
1 tsp fresh ginger, chopped
¼ tsp turmeric
1 tsp salt
½ tsp cayenne pepper (optional)
2 tsp coriander powder
2 tsp lemon juice
½ tsp garam masala
1 tbsp fresh coriander, chopped (cilantro)

1. Trim and divide cauliflower into small 1-inch florets. Rinse and drain well. Set aside.
2. Peel and wash potatoes. Cut into 1-inch pieces. Set aside.
3. Heat 1 tsp oil in a nonstick skillet over medium high heat. Add cumin seeds and fry for a few seconds until seeds are golden brown. Add cauliflower and potatoes. Stir.
4. Add ginger, turmeric, salt and cayenne pepper. Stir thoroughly to coat vegetables.
5. Cover with a lid, heat through and reduce heat. Simmer for 8–10 minutes until vegetables are tender but firm.
6. Sprinkle with coriander powder, lemon juice and garam masala. Stir. Increase heat to medium and pour the remaining 3 tsp of oil around the sides, allowing the oil to get to the bottom of the pan. Fry for 3–5 minutes, stir occasionally in a lifting and turning fashion to avoid

mashing the cauliflower. All the liquid from the vegetables should be evaporated.

7. Transfer to a serving platter. Garnish with fresh coriander, if desired.

Makes 8 servings (4 cups)
Serving size: ½ cup
Amount per serving:
Calories 66
Fat . . . . .2 g
Saturated fat . . . . .0 g
Cholesterol . . . . .0 g

Exchanges: 1 vegetable
½ starch

Carbohydrate . . . . 10 g
Dietary fiber . . . . .1.6 g
Protein . . . . 1 g
Sodium . . . . .272 mg

Bengun

Eggplant with tomatoes and onions

Eggplant is cooked in many different ways—by itself or combined with dal, meat or other vegetables. When available, use the long Chinese eggplant, for it has a milder taste.

1 medium eggplant (¾ lb)

¾ cup thinly sliced onions

1 medium tomato, thinly sliced

4 tsp vegetable oil

¼ tsp cumin seeds

¼ tsp turmeric

½ tsp cayenne pepper (optional)

1 tsp salt

1 small green chili, finely chopped (optional)

2 tsp coriander powder

2 tsp ground fennel seeds

1 tsp lemon juice

1. Divide eggplant into fourths cutting lengthwise and crosswise. Then cut each piece into ¼-inch-thick slices. Set aside. Slice onions and tomatoes and set aside.
2. Heat 1 tsp oil in a nonstick skillet over medium high heat.
3. When oil is hot, add cumin seeds and cook for a few seconds until seeds are golden brown. Add sliced onions, tomatoes and eggplant in that order. Sprinkle turmeric, cayenne pepper, salt, green chili, coriander powder and fennel powder on the eggplant.
4. Stir gently with a spatula in a lifting and turning fashion to coat spices.
5. Cover with a lid. Cook for 10–12 minutes, stirring occasionally as mentioned above. Eggplant is done when it becomes soft to the touch and rather transparent.

5. Open the lid, sprinkle with lemon juice and stir. Pour the remaining 3 tsp of oil around the sides of the pan, allowing the oil to get to the bottom, and fry for another 5–8 minutes. Stir occasionally as before. Transfer to a serving dish.

Makes 6 servings (2 cups)   *Exchanges: 1 vegetable*
Serving size: ⅓ cup   *½ fat*
Amount per serving:

Calories	42	Carbohydrate	3 g
Fat	3 g	Dietary fiber	1 g
Saturated fat	0.4 g	Protein	0.5 g
Cholesterol	0 g	Sodium	358 mg

Sambhara
Sweet-and-sour cabbage

The sweet-and-sour taste of tamarind sauce gives this vegetable a unique taste. This vegetable is a specialty of the state of Gujarat. It goes great with any dal or meat. It is often served with dhokla as a side dish or condiment.

1 medium head cabbage (about 2 lb)
2 carrots, peeled
1 green chili, chopped (optional)
1 cup water
1-inch square of dry tamarind
1 tsp vegetable oil
½ tsp mustard seeds
6–8 curry leaves
¼ tsp turmeric
1½ tsp salt
2 tsp coriander powder
½ tsp cayenne pepper (optional)
2 tbsp firmly packed brown sugar

1. Remove any tough or discolored cabbage leaves and discard. Cut cabbage into fourths. Remove the core and thinly slice cabbage into ¼-inch strips. Peel, wash and julienne (cut into thin strips) the carrots. Set aside.
2. Boil 1 cup water, add tamarind and cook for 2–3 minutes. Remove from the heat and set aside.
3. Heat oil in a heavy skillet or wok over medium heat. When oil is hot, add mustard seeds and curry leaves, covering with a lid to avoid splattering, and cook for a few seconds until the seeds stop popping.
4. Add sliced cabbage, carrots and chopped green chili. Stir.
5. Add turmeric, 1 tsp salt, coriander powder and cayenne pepper. Stir to coat with spices. Cover with a lid and heat through. Reduce heat and

simmer for 5–6 minutes. The cabbage will become transparent and slightly tender.

6. Remove the lid, increase heat and cook for another 3–5 minutes to evaporate any juices that may have accumulated. Remove from the heat.

7. To prepare the tamarind sauce, mash tamarind between fingertips to loosen all the pulp. Strain the tamarind juice and discard any extraneous material. Add brown sugar and ½ tsp salt to the juice. Return it to the stove, bring to a boil and simmer for 3–4 minutes.

8. Add tamarind sauce to the cooked cabbage and stir. Transfer to a serving dish.

Makes 8 servings (4 cups)   *Exchange: 1 vegetable*
Serving size: ½ cup
Amount per serving:

Calories	38	Carbohydrate	8 g
Fat	0.5 g	Dietary fiber	1.7 g
Saturated fat	0 g	Protein	1 g
Cholesterol	0 g	Sodium	416 mg

Bean-moong ki subji
French-style green beans

For a quick and simple way to prepare green beans, try bean-moong ki subji. I use frozen French-style green beans.

1 16-oz frozen French-style green beans
2 tbsp moong dal
1 tsp vegetable oil
½ tsp cumin seeds
½ tsp turmeric
1 tsp salt
2 tsp coriander powder
¼ tsp cayenne pepper (optional)
¾ tsp garam masala
1 tsp lemon juice

1. Thaw green beans. Set aside. Clean moong dal of any extraneous materials and wash in 3–4 changes of water. Set aside.
2. Heat oil in a frying pan over medium high heat. Add cumin seeds and cook for a few seconds until seeds are golden brown. Add the thawed green beans and moong dal. Sprinkle with turmeric and salt and stir to mix. Cover with a lid and heat through. Reduce heat and simmer for 10–12 minutes. Check the moong dal by placing 1–2 dal grains on a plate and pressing with a finger. They should mash easily. Add coriander powder, cayenne pepper, garam masala and lemon juice. Stir to coat the spices. Cook for 2–3 minutes longer to evaporate all the liquid. Transfer to a serving dish.

Makes 6 servings (3 cups)   *Exchange: 1 vegetable*
Serving size: ½ cup
Amount per serving:

Calories	30	Carbohydrate	5 g
Fat	1 g	Dietary fiber	1 g
Saturated fat	0 g	Protein	1 g
Cholesterol	0 g	Sodium	362 mg

Paneer

Fresh cheese

Paneer is increasing in popularity in India. It can be combined with vegetables or made into desserts. I often make the paneer in advance and freeze it. It can be made with low fat or whole milk, but whole milk is preferable because it makes a creamier and firmer cheese. So for best results use whole milk. Nutrient analyses are given for both low fat and whole milk paneer.

8 cups low fat or whole milk
7–9 tsp white vinegar
2 tbsp water

1. Heat milk in a heavy 4-quart saucepan over medium heat. Stir occasionally to avoid scorching on the bottom.
2. In the meantime, mix 7 tsp of vinegar and water and set aside. Place 2 tsp of vinegar in a separate bowl, in case you need it. Place a large strainer over a large bowl. Line the strainer with a thin cloth (large handkerchief) or a double layer of cheesecloth and set aside.
3. When the milk comes to a full boil, reduce heat to a simmer. Gradually add vinegar mixture to a boiling milk and stir gently. Simmer as the cheese (paneer) separates from the whey (greenish yellow liquid). If needed, add 1–2 tsp more vinegar to separate the whey and the paneer. All the paneer is separated when the whey is greenish yellow. Remove from the heat.
4. Pour the entire contents into the cheesecloth. Discard the whey. Rinse paneer with 2 cups of cold water. Gather the cheesecloth so the paneer is in the center. Tie the paneer with one end of the cloth and hang the paneer (a kitchen cabinet door knob works well) to allow the excess liquid to drip for a half hour or longer. Gently squeeze the paneer to remove any liquid.
5. Place the cheese on a clean counter and mix with hands in a kneading motion for 2–3 minutes. The paneer will become crumbly. Gather the

paneer and pat into a rectangular shape about ½-inch-thick. Place it back in the cheesecloth and wrap it. Place between two one-inch thick newspaper stacks and set it on a flat surface. Set a cutting board on top. Now put something heavy (20–30 lb) on top of the cutting board to flatten the paneer. (You can use a 6–8 quart pan filled with water.) Let it rest for 4–6 hours. Unwrap the cheese and cut into ½-inch squares. Refrigerate for up to 2 days until ready to use or freeze for later use.

Whole milk paneer

Makes 2 cups squares   *Exchange: 1 high fat meat*
Serving size: ¼ cup
Amount per serving:
Calories 110   Carbohydrate . . . . 2 g
Fat . . . . .8 g   Dietary fiber. . . . . 0 g
Saturated fat . . . . .5 g   Protein . . . . 8 g
Cholesterol . . . . .33 g   Sodium . . . . .52 mg

Low fat milk paneer

Low fat milk paneer has a slightly softer texture and you may get a little less paneer than with whole milk—but you also get less fat.

Makes 2 cups squares   *Exchange: 1 medium fat meat*
Serving size: ¼ cup
Amount per serving:
Calories 80   Carbohydrate . . . . 2 g
Fat . . . . 4.7 g   Dietary fiber. . . . . 0 g
Saturated fat . . . . .3 g   Protein . . . . 8 g
Cholesterol . . . . .18 g   Sodium . . . . .64 mg

Quick paneer

On days when you are in the mood for paneer and don't have time to make it from scratch, ricotta cheese can be substituted. This paneer is relatively soft. I use part skim ricotta cheese. Just like paneer with whole milk, whole milk ricotta cheese will give you creamier and firmer paneer. The lighter the ricotta cheese, the greater the water content. Fat free ricotta does not make good paneer.

15 oz part skim ricotta cheese

1. Preheat oven to 350° F.
2. Mix ricotta cheese with wire whip to blend well. Place in 8-inch square pan.
3. Bake for 30–35 minutes, until all the liquid is evaporated and cheese is set.
4. Cool completely. Cut into ½-inch squares.

Makes 2 cups squares　　　　*Exchange: 1 medium fat meat*
Serving size: ¼ cup
Amount per serving:

Calories 73	Carbohydrate . . . . 3 g
Fat . . . . 4.0 g	Dietary fiber . . . . 0 g
Saturated fat . . . . 2.5 g	Protein . . . . 6 g
Cholesterol . . . . 16 g	Sodium . . . . .66 mg

Matar paneer
Pea and cheese curry

Matar paneer makes any meal special. Traditionally the paneer squares were deep-fat fried to a golden brown before adding them to the sauce. I don't fry the paneer and find the taste much more appealing.

1 medium onion, peeled and cut into 8 pieces
1 tsp fresh ginger, chopped
½ cup tomato sauce
2 tbsp vegetable oil
½ tsp cumin seeds
⅓ cup plain nonfat yogurt
¼ tsp turmeric
2 tsp coriander powder
½ tsp cayenne pepper (optional)
3 cups water
2 cups frozen peas
1 tsp salt
1 cup paneer pieces, made with low fat milk
   (see recipe Paneer on page 197)
¾ tsp garam masala
2 tbsp chopped fresh coriander leaves (cilantro)

1. In a blender jar grind onion and ginger to a smooth paste. Set aside.
2. Heat 1 tbsp oil in a nonstick skillet over medium high heat. Add cumin seeds and cook for a few seconds until seeds are golden brown. Add onion mixture. Cook until most of the liquid has evaporated. Add the remaining 1 tbsp oil and cook until onions are golden brown, stirring as needed to avoid sticking and burning. Stir in tomato sauce and continue to cook.
3. Whip yogurt with a fork until it is smooth. Gradually add yogurt, 1 tbsp at a time, to the onion mixture, stirring constantly. Add turmeric, coriander powder and cayenne pepper. Continue to cook until most of the

liquid evaporates and the mixture is thick enough to draw away from the sides and bottom of the pan in a dense mass.

4. Add water, peas and salt. Bring to a boil, cover with a lid, reduce heat and simmer for 10 minutes. Add paneer and simmer for another 5–7 minutes.
5. Add garam masala and stir. Let stand until ready to serve. Transfer to a serving dish and garnish with fresh coriander, if desired.

Makes 4 cups (8 servings)   *Exchanges: 1 high fat meat*
Serving size: ½ cup   *½ starch*
Amount per serving:

Calories	143	Carbohydrate	9 g
Fat	8 g	Dietary fiber	2 g
Saturated fat	3 g	Protein	9 g
Cholesterol	15 g	Sodium	524 mg

Palak paneer
Spinach with cheese

Whether or not you like spinach, this dish is a must try. I always use frozen spinach for this recipe.

1 lb spinach, fresh or frozen (chopped)
1 small onion, cut into 4 pieces
1 tsp fresh ginger, chopped
1 tsp salt
½ tsp turmeric
½ tsp cayenne pepper (optional)
1 cup water
1½ cups paneer, made with low fat milk (see recipe Paneer on page 197)
1 tsp vegetable oil
½ tsp cumin seeds

1. In a heavy skillet, mix the spinach, onion, ginger, salt, turmeric, cayenne pepper and ½ cup water. Bring to a boil, reduce heat, cover with a lid and steam for 5 minutes or until greens are soft. Set aside to cool.
2. In a blender jar add the cooled spinach mixture and coarsely grind.
3. Return the coarsely ground spinach to the skillet and stir in the remaining water. Cover with a lid and cook on medium heat until spinach is simmering. (VERY IMPORTANT: Before stirring, remove the skillet from the heat and carefully remove the lid. The spinach tends to splatter and can burn.) Reduce heat and simmer for 20–30 minutes. A longer cooking time adds flavor to the spinach.
4. Remove spinach from the heat, add paneer and stir. Cover with a lid and return to the stove. Continue to simmer for 8–10 minutes. Remove from the heat.
5. To prepare chounk (seasoning): In a separate small fry pan heat oil on medium heat, add cumin seeds and cook for a few seconds until seeds turn golden brown.

6. Carefully add the chounk to the spinach, stir and cover with a lid. Let stand until ready to serve.

Makes 8 servings (4 cups)
Serving size: ½ cup
Amount per serving:

Calories	122	
Fat	.7 g	
Saturated fat	.4 g	
Cholesterol	21 g	

Exchanges: 1 high fat meat
1 vegetable

Carbohydrate	5 g
Dietary fiber	1.3 g
Protein	11 g
Sodium	492 mg

Sukhi subji

Frozen mixed vegetables

When in a hurry, frozen mixed vegetables can be a lifesaver.

1 tsp vegetable oil
¼ tsp cumin seeds
1 16 oz. package of frozen mixed vegetables
¼ tsp turmeric
2 tsp coriander powder
½ tsp salt
¼ tsp cayenne pepper (optional)
¼ cup water
1 tsp garam masala
1 tsp lemon juice

1. Heat oil in a nonstick skillet over medium high heat. Add cumin seeds and cook for a few seconds until seeds turn golden brown.
2. Add frozen vegetables, turmeric, salt, coriander powder, cayenne pepper and water. Stir well. Heat through, cover with a lid and simmer for 8–9 minutes till vegetables are tender, stirring occasionally.
3. Add garam masala and lemon juice. If there is any liquid left, increase heat and cook for a few minutes to evaporate it. Transfer to a serving dish.

Makes 4 servings (2 cups)
Serving size: ½ cup
Amount per serving:

Calories	65	Carbohydrate	12 g
Fat	1 g	Dietary fiber	2 g
Saturated fat	0 g	Protein	3 g
Cholesterol	0 g	Sodium	300 mg

Exchanges: 1 vegetable
½ starch

Sukhi matar

Spicy peas

I remember shelling fresh peas as a family affair. I now enjoy the convenience of frozen peas. Serve this dish with an Indian or a Western meal.

1 medium onion
1 tbsp vegetable oil
½ tsp cumin seeds
1 (16 oz) package frozen peas, thawed
¼ tsp turmeric
¼ tsp cayenne pepper (optional)
1 tbsp coriander powder
¾ tsp salt
2 tbsp water
½ tsp garam masala

1. Peel and grate onion. Set aside.
2. Heat oil in a heavy nonstick skillet on medium heat. Add cumin seeds and cook for a few seconds until seeds are golden brown.
3. Add grated onions and cook until lightly browned.
4. Add thawed peas, turmeric, cayenne pepper, coriander powder, salt and water. Stir. Cover with a lid and heat through. Reduce heat and simmer for 10 minutes.
5. Stir in garam masala and cook for another 3–5 minutes, stirring occasionally. Evaporate any excess liquid. Transfer to a serving dish.

Makes 5 servings (2½ cups)
Serving size: ½ cup
Amount per serving:

Exchanges: 1 starch
½ fat

Calories 93	Carbohydrate . . . . 13 g
Fat . . . . 3 g	Dietary fiber . . . . 3.3 g
Saturated fat . . . . 0.4 g	Protein . . . . 4 g
Cholesterol . . . . 0 g	Sodium . . . . 390 mg

Sag

Mixed greens

Sag is a very popular dish from the state of Punjab. It tastes great with wheat or corn roti. Traditionally, it is cooked for hours to blend and to acquire a savory taste, but I use frozen greens and grind them in a blender to get the same taste with much less time and effort.

1 lb mustard greens, cleaned and chopped
   or 1 lb frozen chopped mustard greens
10 oz spinach, cleaned and chopped
   or 10 oz. frozen chopped spinach
1 small onion, peeled and cut into 8 pieces
1 tsp ginger, chopped
½ tsp turmeric
½ tsp cayenne pepper (optional)
1½ tsp salt
3 cup water
3 tbsp cornmeal
2 tsp vegetable oil
½ tsp cumin seeds
2 red dry whole chilies (optional)

1. In a heavy skillet, add the chopped greens, onion, ginger, turmeric, salt and 1 cup water. Steam for 10 minute. Set aside to cool.
2. In a blender jar, put the greens and grind coarsely. Grind half of the greens at a time and use the water as needed.
3. Return pureed greens to the skillet. Cover and bring to a boil. Reduce heat and simmer, stirring occasionally. (VERY IMPORTANT: Before stirring, remove the skillet from the heat, and carefully remove the lid. The sag tends to splatter and can burn.)
4. Mix cornmeal in ¼ cup water. Carefully add to the greens and stir to mix thoroughly. Simmer for 20 minutes. Remove from the heat.

5. To prepare chounk (seasoning): Heat oil in a small fry pan oven medium Add cumin seeds and red chilies and cook for a few seconds until seeds turn golden brown. With lid to the sag in one hand, carefully add chounk to the pureed greens and then cover with the lid. Transfer to a serving dish.

Makes 12 servings (6 cups)   *Exchange: 1 vegetable*
Serving size: ½ cup
Amount per serving:
Calories 28   Carbohydrate . . . . 4 g
Fat . . . . .1 g   Dietary fiber . . . . .1.7 g
Saturated fat . . . . .0 g   Protein . . . . 2 g
Cholesterol . . . . .0 g   Sodium . . . . .290 mg

Alu tari

Potato curry

Quick and easy way to prepare potatoes. Can be made with boiled or raw potatoes. Serve with chapati or bread.

3 medium potatoes, boiled
1 tsp oil
¼ tsp cumin seeds
½ tsp turmeric
2 tsp coriander powder
¼ tsp cayenne pepper (optional)
¾ tsp salt
2 cups water
½ tsp garam masala
1tsp lemon juice
1 tbsp chopped fresh coriander (cilantro)

1. Peel potatoes and break them into small pieces ½–1-inch pieces. Set aside.
2. Heat oil in a heavy saucepan over medium heat. Add cumin seeds and cook for a few seconds until the seeds are golden brown.
3. Add potatoes and stir. Stir in turmeric, coriander powder, cayenne pepper, salt and water. Bring to a boil. Reduce heat, cover with a lid and simmer for 12–15 minutes.
4. Add garam masala and lemon juice. Transfer to a serving dish and garnish with fresh coriander, if desired.

Makes 6 servings (3 cups)   *Exchange: 1 starch*
Serving size: ½ cup
Amount per serving:
Calories 70   Carbohydrate . . . . 15 g
Fat . . . . 1 g   Dietary fiber . . . . 1 g
Saturated fat . . . . 0 g   Protein . . . . 1 g
Cholesterol . . . . 0 g   Sodium . . . . .270 mg

Chicken is the most-popular meat served in India. It can be prepared in a simple manner or an elegant one fit for a king. In India the skin is always removed from the chicken before it is cooked. In most Indian dishes the chicken is cut into small parts. The drumsticks and thighs are separated. The breast is cut into four to eight parts. I used only chicken parts instead of a whole chicken for the recipes in this cookbook as chicken parts are easier and faster to cook. I usually have the butcher skin the chicken and cut it into 2–3-inch pieces.

Once the skin is removed, chicken is a very lean choice. I have used both white and dark meat for my recipes, allowing for more flexibility in a family meal. White meat is the leanest of chicken parts. The dark meat is slightly higher in fat than white meat but still quite lean.

Traditionally, chicken is often marinated in spices, stir-fried in oil, added to the fried spice mixture (masala) and cooked or simmered to make the sauce (curry). A fair amount of oil is used. I have used as little oil as possible to maintain the flavor, texture and taste. The recipes are, therefore, much lower in fat than the traditional recipes but the taste is unaltered.

Enjoy them—from the very lean marinated tandoori chicken to the rich mughlai chicken. Chicken is usually served with rice, naan or roti. Serve it with salad and/or a vegetable to make an elegant and balanced meal.

For the nutrient analysis I have used approximately half white and half dark meat to give a representative average. However, some recipes do call for white meat only. So for calculating exchanges, the calories may be less than the exchanges compute as lean meat is based on 3 grams of fat and white meat has only 1 gram of fat.

Kali mirch murgh
Blackened chicken

This is a quick, low fat recipe using just white meat. If you like the flavor of black pepper, you will love this dish. This also tastes great in sandwiches.

2 lb chicken breasts, skinned and deboned
1 tsp fresh ginger, chopped
2 garlic clove, chopped
1 tsp salt
1 tsp black pepper, coarsely ground
1 tsp vegetable oil
1 tbsp lemon juice

1. Cut chicken breast into 1–2-inch pieces. (Cut chicken breast in half for sandwiches.) Rub chicken pieces with ginger, garlic, salt and black pepper and set aside.
2. Heat the oil in a wok or a nonstick skillet over medium high heat, coating the pan with oil by shaking it. When the oil is hot, add chicken and stir-fry for 10 minutes. Cover with a lid, reduce heat and simmer for 10–12 minutes until chicken is tender.
3. Transfer to a serving platter and sprinkle with lemon juice.

Makes 6 servings
Serving size: ⅙ recipe
Amount per serving:

Exchanges: 3 lean meat

Calories 125	Carbohydrate . . . . 0 g
Fat .3 g	Dietary fiber . . . . 0 g
Saturated fat . . . . .1 g	Protein . . . . 22 g
Cholesterol . . . . .60 g	Sodium . . . . .408 mg

Tandoori murgh
Barbecued chicken

An elegant dish from the state of Punjab, tantoori murgh is one of the most-popular chicken dishes. It can be made in a tandoor (clay oven), baked in an oven or grilled on a barbecue.

3 lb chicken pieces
1 small onion
½ cup tomato sauce
½ cup nonfat plain yogurt
1 tsp fresh ginger, chopped
2 garlic cloves
2 tsp coriander powder
½ tsp cayenne pepper (optional)
2 whole cloves
1 tsp cumin seeds
4 cardamom pods
1 tsp salt
1 tsp garam masala
¼ tsp red food coloring

1. Remove the skin and all visible fat from the chicken pieces. (I often have the butcher skin the chicken.) Cut 2–3 slits, 1 inch long and ½ inch deep, in each piece of chicken. Place in a casserole dish and set aside.
2. Cut onion into 4–6 pieces. In a blender jar put onion, tomato sauce, yogurt, ginger, garlic cloves, coriander powder, cayenne pepper, cloves, cumin seeds, cardamom pods, salt, garam masala and red food coloring. Blend to a smooth paste.
3. Pour the tandoori paste on the chicken and turn pieces to thoroughly coat with spices. Cover with a lid or plastic wrap and marinate in the refrigerator 4–24 hours.
4. Preheat the oven to 400° F. Remove chicken pieces from the marinade, saving marinade. Arrange pieces in a broiler pan. Bake uncovered in the

middle of the oven for 30 minutes. Turn pieces over and brush with remaining marinade. Bake for 10–15 minutes until chicken is tender.

. Turn oven to broil. Turn pieces over once again and broil for 5 minutes to get a nice red color.

. Transfer to a serving platter. Serve with lemon wedges or squeeze lemon juice over the chicken before eating, if desired.

Makes 6 servings
Serving size: ⅙ recipe
Amount per serving:

Exchanges: 3 lean meat

Calories 155	Carbohydrate . . . . 4 g
Fat . . . . 4 g	Dietary fiber . . . . 0.5 g
Saturated fat . . . . 1 g	Protein . . . . 24 g
Cholesterol . . . . 66 g	Sodium . . . . 551 mg

Murgh tar(

Chicken curry

Murgh tari is the most-common way to serve chicken. The curry (sauce) tastes great with roti or rice. Typically a large amount of oil is used in preparing the sauce. However, by using a nonstick skillet and all the spices, you can reduce the fat significantly without altering the taste.

3 lb chicken pieces
2 tbsp vegetable oil
1 tsp cumin powder
4 cardamom pods
1 2-inch piece of cinnamon stick
1 medium onion, finely chopped
4 garlic cloves, chopped
2 tsp fresh ginger, chopped
1 medium tomato, finely chopped
½ tsp turmeric
1 tbsp coriander powder
½ tsp cayenne pepper (optional)
½ tsp fennel seeds, coarsely ground
1 tsp black pepper, coarsely ground
½ cup plain nonfat yogurt
1 tsp salt
½ cup water
2 tbsp chopped fresh coriander (cilantro)
1 tbsp fresh lemon juice

1. Remove the skin and all visible fat from the chicken pieces. (I often have the butcher clean the chicken.) Cut 2–3 slits, 1 inch long and ½ inch deep, in each piece of chicken. Set aside.
2. Heat oil in a heavy skillet over medium high heat. Add the chicken pieces in a single layer and fry for 3–5 minutes, turning the pieces over

once or twice until they are white. Transfer the chicken to a plate using a slotted spoon.

. Add cumin powder, cardamom pods, cinnamon stick, chopped onion, garlic and ginger to the oil. Fry for 7–8 minutes, stirring constantly, until the onions are golden brown.

. Stir in tomatoes, turmeric, coriander powder, cayenne pepper, ground fennel seeds and black pepper. Fry for 2–3 minutes. Whip yogurt with wire wisk and add 1 tbsp at a time, stirring constantly. Fry for another 2–4 minutes.

. Add the chicken and sprinkle with salt. Stir to coat the spice mixture evenly. Pour the water evenly over the chicken. Bring to a boil. Reduce heat to low. Add the fresh coriander and gently stir the chicken. Cover tightly and simmer for 20–25 minutes. Chicken should be tender to the touch but should not fall apart.

. Transfer to a serving platter. Sprinkle with lemon juice.

Makes 6 servings
Serving size: ⅙ recipe
Amount per serving:

Exchanges: 3½ lean meat

Calories	197	Carbohydrate	4 g
Fat	9 g	Dietary fiber	0.7 g
Saturated fat	1.8 g	Protein	24 g
Cholesterol	67 g	Sodium	430 mg

Murgh subji wala

Chicken with vegetables

Served with rice or naan, murgh subji wala makes a complete and very tasty meal.

3 lb chicken pieces
2 tbsp vegetable oil
1 tsp cumin powder
1 medium onion, thinly sliced
2 garlic cloves, chopped
1 tsp fresh ginger, chopped
1 large bell pepper, sliced into ¼-inch-thick strips
2 medium tomatoes, sliced into ½-inch wedges
¾ cup mushrooms, thinly sliced
¼ tsp turmeric
¼ tsp cayenne pepper (optional)
2 tsp coriander powder
1½ tsp salt
½ tsp garam masala

1. Remove the skin and all visible fat from the chicken pieces. (I often have the butcher clean the chicken.) Cut 2–3 slits, 1 inch long and ½ inch deep, in each piece of chicken. Set aside.
2. Heat oil in a heavy skillet over medium high heat. Add the chicken pieces in a single layer and fry for 3–5 minutes, turning the pieces over once or twice until they are white. Transfer the chicken to a plate using a slotted spoon.
3. Add cumin powder, sliced onions, garlic and ginger. Fry for 7–8 minutes, stirring constantly until the onions are golden brown.
4. Add the sliced bell peppers, tomatoes, mushrooms, turmeric, cayenne pepper, coriander powder and salt. Stir thoroughly.
5. Add the chicken, stirring to mix. Heat through, cover with a lid and reduce heat. Simmer for about 20–25 minutes until chicken is tender.

6. Remove from the heat and sprinkle with garam masala. Cover with a lid and let stand until ready to serve.

Makes 6 servings   *Exchanges: 3 lean meat*
Serving size: ⅙ recipe   *1 vegetable*
Amount per serving:

Calories 193   Carbohydrate . . . . 4 g
Fat . . . . .9 g   Dietary fiber . . . . 1 g
Saturated fat . . . . 1.8 g   Protein . . . . 23 g
Cholesterol . . . . .67 g   Sodium . . . . .595 mg

Murgh khorma
Chicken in yogurt sauce

I often make this when I am in a hurry because it does not need to be marinated— a quick and delicious way to prepare chicken.

3 lb chicken parts
½ cup plain nonfat yogurt
1 tsp fresh ginger, chopped
2 garlic cloves, chopped
2 tsp garam masala
½ tsp cayenne pepper (optional)
1 tsp coriander powder
1 tsp salt
2 tbsp vegetable oil
½ tsp cumin seeds
1 medium onion, thinly sliced
½ cup water
1 green chili, chopped (optional)
2 tbsp chopped fresh coriander

1. Remove the skin and all visible fat from the chicken pieces. Cut into 8–10 pieces. (I will often have the butcher do this for me.) Cut 2–3 slits, 1 inch long and ½ inch deep, in each piece of chicken. Set aside.
2. In a small bowl mix yogurt, chopped ginger, garlic, garam masala, cayenne pepper, coriander powder and salt. Pour over chicken and mix well.
3. Heat oil in a heavy skillet. When oil is hot, add cumin seeds and cook for a few seconds until seeds are golden brown. Add sliced onions. Fry onions until golden brown, stirring as needed.
4. Add chicken along with the marinade and fry for 8–10 minutes. Add the water, chopped green chili and fresh coriander and stir well. Cover with a lid and reduce heat. Simmer for 20–25 minutes. Stir occasionally. Transfer to a serving dish.

Makes 6 servings
Serving size: ⅙ recipe
Amount per serving:

Calories 193	Carbohydrate . . . . 3 g
Fat . . . . .9 g	Dietary fiber . . . . 0 g
Saturated fat . . . . 1.8 g	Protein . . . . 23 g
Cholesterol . . . . .67 g	Sodium . . . . .428 mg

Exchanges: 3½ lean meat

Mughlai murgh
Chicken with almonds and raisins

Chicken fit for a king! The original version is cooked with cream and a fair amount of oil, but you will not miss the cream or the fat in this recipe. It is great for parties.

3 lb chicken parts
1 large onion, cut into 8 pieces
1-inch fresh ginger
4 garlic cloves
½ tsp cayenne pepper (optional)
1 tsp coriander powder
1 cup nonfat yogurt
2 tbsp vegetable oil
1 tsp cumin seeds
4 cardamom pods
2 bay leaves
1-inch cinnamon stick
4 whole cloves
¼ cup water
1 tsp salt
2 tbsp golden raisins
¼ cup blanched, slivered almonds
½ tsp garam masala
2 tbsp chopped fresh coriander

1. Remove the skin and all visible fat from the chicken pieces. Cut into 8–10 pieces. (I will often have the butcher clean the chicken.) Cut 2–3 slits, 1 inch long and ½ inch deep, in each piece of chicken. Set aside.
2. In a blender grind onion, ginger and garlic. Set aside.
3. Heat oil in a heavy skillet over medium high heat. Add the chicken pieces in a single layer and fry for 3–5 minutes, turning the pieces over

once or twice until they are white. Transfer the chicken to a plate using a slotted spoon.

4. In the same oil add cumin seeds, cardamom pods, bay leaves, cinnamon stick and cloves. Fry for a few seconds until cumin seeds turn golden brown. Add the onion paste and fry again until golden brown. Whip yogurt with a fork and gradually add 1 tbsp at a time to the onion masala, stirring continuously until all the yogurt is well blended. Continue to cook until most of the liquid is evaporated and the mixture draws into a dense mass.

5. Add chicken and any juices that may have accumulated. Stir thoroughly. Add water and salt and mix again. Bring to a boil, reduce heat, cover with a lid and simmer for 20–25 minutes.

6. In the meantime heat oven to 300° F. Put the almonds in a baking dish and roast them until light brown (15–20 minutes), shaking the pan frequently to avoid burning.

7. Add the raisins to the chicken, stir thoroughly, cover and simmer for 10 minutes. Add 2 tbsp of the roasted almonds, garam masala and chopped coriander and stir gently.

8. Transfer to a serving platter and garnish with the remaining roasted almonds before serving.

Makes 6 servings
Serving size: ⅙ recipe
Amount per serving:

		Exchanges: 3 medium fat meat	
		½ starch	
Calories	241	Carbohydrate	8 g
Fat	11 g	Dietary fiber	1 g
Saturated fat	2 g	Protein	26 g
Cholesterol	67 g	Sodium	443 mg

Murgh sag wala
Chicken with spinach

Served with rice or naan murgh sag wala makes a complete meal. When in a hurry use frozen spinach and have the butcher skin and chop the chicken for an easy-to-fix chicken dish.

2½ lb chicken parts
2 packages (10 oz each) frozen chopped spinach, thawed
2 tbsp vegetable oil
1 tsp cumin seeds
1 medium onion, finely chopped
1 tsp fresh ginger, chopped
2 garlic cloves, chopped
½ tsp turmeric
½ tsp cayenne pepper (optional)
2 tsp coriander powder
1½ tsp salt
1 tsp garam masala
2 tbsp fresh lemon juice

1. Remove the skin and all visible fat from the chicken pieces. Cut chicken into 2 inch pieces. (I often have the butcher clean the chicken.) Set aside.
2. Chop fresh spinach or squeeze thawed frozen spinach lightly between hands to remove excess water. Set aside.
3. Heat oil in a nonstick skillet over medium high heat. Add the chicken pieces in a single layer and fry for 3–5 minutes, turning the pieces over once or twice until they are white. Transfer the chicken to a plate using a slotted spoon.
4. In the same oil add cumin seeds and cook for a few seconds until seeds are golden brown. Add chopped onion, ginger and garlic. Fry until the onions are lightly brown.
5. Add the spinach and stir. Then add the turmeric, chili, coriander powder and salt; stir thoroughly.

5. Add the chicken, stirring to mix. Cover with a lid, heat through and reduce the heat. Simmer for 20–25 minutes, stirring occasionally. Uncover and increase heat to evaporate any excess liquid.

7. Remove from the heat and sprinkle with garam masala and lemon juice. Cover with a lid and let stand until ready to serve.

Makes 6 servings
Serving size: ⅙ recipe
Amount per serving:

Calories	175	Carbohydrate	6 g
Fat	8 g	Dietary fiber	2 g
Saturated fat	1.5 g	Protein	21 g
Cholesterol	52 g	Sodium	652 mg

Exchanges: 3 lean meat
1 vegetable

Mysore murgh
Stir-fried chicken

As the name states, this dish is from the state of Mysore. The seasonings of urd dal and fennel seeds give this dish a very unique flavor. The bones are usually not removed as they add flavor to the dish. If you choose, you can use boneless chicken breasts for this recipe and the fat content will then be lower.

3 lb chicken parts
1 tsp salt
¼ tsp turmeric
1 tbsp vegetable oil
½ tsp mustard seeds
½ tsp urd dal
½ tsp fennel seeds
3 whole dried red chilies
1 large onion, finely chopped
3 tbsp water

1. Remove the skin and all visible fat from the chicken pieces. Cut chicken in to 2 inch pieces. (I often will have the butcher do this for me.) Rub salt and turmeric on the chicken pieces. Set aside.
2. Heat the oil in a wok or a fry pan over medium high heat. Add mustard seeds, cover with a lid to avoid splattering and cook for a few seconds until the seeds stop popping. Add the dal, fennel seeds and red chilies. Fry for a few seconds until the chilies darken. Add the chopped onions. Fry until light brown.
3. Add the chicken and fry for about 5 minutes, stirring constantly. Add water about 1 tbsp at a time while continuing to stir. Cook for another 10–12 minutes. The chicken should be tender and slightly brown.
4. Transfer to a serving platter and garnish with the marinated onions and sliced tomatoes (see recipe Piaz aur tamatar ka salad on page 264), if desired.

Makes 6 servings
Serving size: ⅙ recipe
Amount per serving:

Calories 162

Fat . . . . 7 g

Saturated fat . . . . 1.5 g

Cholesterol . . . . 66 g

Exchanges: 3 lean meat

Carbohydrate . . . . 2 g

Dietary fiber . . . . 0 g

Protein . . . . 23 g

Sodium . . . . 414 mg

Dhania murgh
Coriander chicken

The coriander leaves give this dish a fresh flavor. Combined with tomatoes and green pepper it makes a very colorful and tasty dish.

3 lb chicken, skinned and deboned
1 tsp salt
1 inch fresh ginger
2 garlic cloves
1 medium onion
1 cup fresh coriander leaves
1 green chili (optional)
2 medium tomatoes
2 medium peppers
2 tbsp vegetable oil

1. Cut chicken into 2 inch pieces. Season with salt. (I often have the butcher skin, debone and cut the chicken.) Set aside.
2. In a blender grind ginger, garlic, onion, coriander leaves and green chili to a smooth paste. Add to chicken and marinate for 20–30 minutes at room temperature.
3. Cut tomatoes and green peppers into 1-inch pieces. Set aside.
4. Coat wok or a skillet with oil and heat over medium high heat. When the oil is hot, add chicken with the marinade and stir-fry for 8–10 minutes, stirring constantly. Add tomatoes and green peppers and stir. Cover with a lid and simmer for 10 minutes. Transfer to a serving dish.

Makes 6 servings
Serving size: ⅙ recipe
Amount per serving:

		Exchanges: 3 lean meat	
		1 vegetable	
Calories	176	Carbohydrate	5 g
Fat	7 g	Dietary fiber	1.4 g
Saturated fat	1.5 g	Protein	23 g
Cholesterol	66 g	Sodium	418 mg

Fish

In India the states of Bengal and Kerala are known for their fish dishes. The important thing to remember about fish is the fresher the fish, the better the taste. Make sure the fish you buy is fresh, preferably caught the same day. It should be shiny with good color, firm to the touch and mild and fresh in aroma. Do not buy dull or faded fish or ones that have a pronounced "fishy" smell. If fresh fish is not available, frozen fish can be used. Nevers overcook fish.

Fish is often breaded, fried and/or curried for Indian dishes. Breaded and fried fish are not included in this book. A minimum amount of oil is used in preparation. The fat content is kept very low without compromising any of the taste.

Flounder, cod, halibut, orange roughy or perch work well for Indian dishes. These varieties are naturally low in fat and calories so you can enjoy trying the following tasty recipes.

For nutritional analysis, cod has been used. For calculating the exchanges, the calories may be less than the exchanges state as lean meat is based on three grams of fat and fish has about one gram of fat per ounce.

Machhi kali mirch
Baked fish with black pepper

For a quick and easy way to cook fish, try machhi kali mirch. If desired, marinate the fish the night before and refrigerate it. You can either bake it or stir-fry it in a pan.

2 lb fish fillets
1 tsp salt
¼ tsp turmeric
1 tsp cumin powder
1 tsp ground black pepper
2 garlic cloves, chopped
2 tsp oil
1 tbsp fresh lemon juice

1. Place fish fillets in a bowl, sprinkle with salt, turmeric, cumin powder, black pepper and garlic; toss to coat well. Cover and marinate for 20 minutes at room temperature or longer in the refrigerator.
2. Preheat over to 400° F. Coat the bottom of baking dish with the oil. Place the fish in a single layer and pour the marinade over it. Bake uncovered for 20–25 minutes. The fish should be firm to the touch. Fish is done when it easily flakes with a fork. Sprinkle with lemon juice.

Makes 8 servings
Serving size: ⅛ recipe
Amount per serving:

Calories	119	Carbohydrate	0 g
Fat	2.5 g	Dietary fiber	0 g
Saturated fat	0.5 g	Protein	22 g
Cholesterol	40 g	Sodium	315 mg

Exchanges: 3 lean meat

Machhi tari

Fish curry

Meat or vegetables in a sauce (curry) is a very popular way to prepare food. The curry tastes good with rice or roti. This is a lightly seasoned fish in a curry. Choose the fish of your choice.

1½ lb fish fillets

½ tsp turmeric

¼ tsp cayenne pepper (optional)

1 tsp salt

2 tbsp vegetable oil

1 medium onion, cut into 8 pieces

1 inch fresh ginger

2 garlic cloves

1 large tomato, chopped

½ tsp cumin powder

1 tsp coriander powder

¼ cup plain nonfat yogurt

1 cup water

1. Cut the fish fillets into 3–4-inch pieces. Sprinkle with turmeric, cayenne pepper and salt. Coat the fish fillets evenly with the spices. Set aside.
2. In a blender jar grind onion, ginger and garlic to a paste. Set aside.
3. Heat 1 tbsp oil in a nonstick skillet over medium high heat. Add fish pieces in a single layer and cook for 1 minute on each side. Remove with slotted spoon and set aside.
4. Add onion paste and cook until most of the liquid is evaporated. Add the remaining 1 tbsp oil and fry until the onions are light brown.
5. Reduce heat to medium. Add chopped tomatoes, cumin powder and coriander powder. Fry for 3–5 minutes. Whip yogurt lightly and add 1 tbsp at a time, stirring constantly. Cook until most of the liquid is evaporated and the onion masala draws into a dense mass.

6. Add the fish pieces, stirring gently to coat the spice mixture. Pour the water evenly over the fish. Bring to a boil. Reduce heat to low. Cover tightly and simmer for 5–7 minutes.
7. Transfer to a serving platter. Sprinkle with chopped coriander, if desired.

Makes 6 servings
Serving size: ⅙ recipe
Amount per serving:

Exchanges: 3 lean meat

Calories 155	Carbohydrate . . . . 3 g
Fat . . . . .6 g	Dietary fiber . . . . 0 g
Saturated fat . . . . 0.8 g	Protein . . . . 22 g
Cholesterol . . . . .45 g	Sodium . . . . .432 mg

Machhi aur ghia
Fish with zucchini

Fish is often cooked with a variety of vegetables for a change of flavor and taste. In India we use bottle gourd for this recipe but zucchini is a great substitute.

1½ lb fish fillets
2 zucchini (1 lb)
3 medium size firm tomatoes
   or 1 cup chopped canned tomatoes, drained
1 tbsp oil
1 tsp cumin powder
2 garlic cloves, chopped
1 tsp fresh ginger, chopped
½ tsp cayenne pepper (optional)
½ tsp turmeric
1 tsp salt
1 tbsp fresh coriander, finely chopped
1 tbsp fresh lemon juice

1. In a bowl coat fish with cumin powder, garlic, ginger, cayenne pepper and turmeric. Set aside. Cut tomatoes and zucchini into 1-inch squares. Set aside.
2. Heat oil in a heavy nonstick skillet over medium heat. Add fish and fry on each side for 1–2 minutes.
3. Add zucchini and tomatoes, sprinkle with salt and stir in a lifting motion to blend in the spices. Bring to a boil, cover with a lid and simmer for 4–5 minutes. Uncover, add chopped fresh coriander and lemon juice and stir gently. Increase heat to evaporate any excess liquid until the sauce thickens and clings to the fish and vegetables.
4. Transfer to a serving platter.

Amount per serving:

Calories 148	Carbohydrate . . . . 4 g
Fat . . . . .4 g	Dietary fiber . . . . .1.5 g
Saturated fat . . . . 0.6 g	Protein . . . . 23 g
Cholesterol . . . . .40 g	Sodium . . . . .409 mg

Sarson wali machhi

Fish in mustard sauce

The state of Bengal is famous for its fish. In Bengal fish is generally prepared in mustard oil. This is a simple dish that can be marinated ahead of time and microwaved or baked when ready to serve.

1½ lb fish fillets
1 tsp salt
½ tsp turmeric
¼ cup mustard seeds
¾ cup water

1. Place fish in a microwave-safe container in a single layer. Sprinkle ½ tsp salt and ¼ tsp turmeric on the fish and rub in. Set aside.
2. Grind mustard seeds, the remaining salt and turmeric with water to a fine paste.
3. Pour mustard paste on fish, covering both sides.
4. Cover with plastic wrap. Marinate for 20 minutes at room temperature or longer in the refrigerator (it can be marinated overnight).
5. Microwave on high for 5 minutes, turn the dish 90° F angle and microwave for 4–7 minutes longer. Fish should be firm to the touch and flake easily when touched with a fork.

Makes 6 servings   *Exchanges: 3 lean meat*
Serving size: ⅙ recipe
Amount per serving:

Calories 139	Carbohydrate . . . . 2 g
Fat . . . . .3 g	Dietary fiber . . . . 0 g
Saturated fat . . . . 0.4 g	Protein . . . . 24 g
Cholesterol . . . . .40 g	Sodium . . . . .404 mg

Tandoori jhinga
Barbecued shrimp

A popular dish with both adults and children, tandoori jhinga adds a special touch to any barbecue party.

1 lb shrimp, medium or large
¾ cup nonfat plain yogurt
1 tsp garlic, finely chopped
1 tsp fresh ginger, grated
1 tsp garam masala
½ tsp salt
1 tsp black pepper, freshly ground
1 tsp red coloring (optional)

1. Shell and devein the shrimp. Butterfly them by slicing lengthwise from the head to the tail, leaving the ends intact. Set aside.
2. In a medium glass bowl, mix the yogurt, garlic, ginger, garam masala, salt, black pepper and coloring. Blend thoroughly. Add the shrimp and marinate for 2–6 hours in the refrigerator.
3. Barbecue on a grill or broil in a preheated oven.
4. Thread 5–6 shrimps on each lightly oiled skewer. Grill or broil for 5–7 minutes on each side until lightly blackened. Serve directly on skewers or remove from skewers and place on a bed of rice or lettuce.

Makes 4 servings
Serving size: ¼ recipe
Amount per serving:

Exchanges: 1½ lean meat

Calories 65	Carbohydrate . . . . 3 g
Fat . . . . 0.5 g	Dietary fiber . . . . 0 g
Saturated fat . . . . 0.2 g	Protein . . . . 11 g
Cholesterol . . . . 83 g	Sodium . . . . .394 mg

Tamatari jhinga
Shrimp with tomatoes

If you are in a hurry, buy frozen, deveined shrimp and use canned tomatoes. The sweet-and-sour taste often makes this a favorite of children.

1 lb jumbo shrimp
2 tbsp fresh lemon juice
1 tsp ground cumin
¼ tsp turmeric
¼ tsp cayenne pepper
¼ tsp black pepper, coarsely ground
1 tsp salt
2 tbsp vegetable oil
½ tsp brown mustard seeds
1 medium onion, finely chopped
1 tsp chopped fresh ginger
2 garlic cloves, finely chopped
6 medium, firm tomatoes, cut into 1-inch squares
  or 2 cups chopped canned tomatoes, drained
1 tbsp jaggery or brown sugar
2 tbsp fresh coriander, chopped

1. Shell and devein shrimp. Wash and pat dry. Place in a medium bowl. In a separate bowl add lemon juice, ground cumin, turmeric, cayenne pepper, black pepper and ½ tsp salt. Mix well with a fork. Pour over shrimp and toss well. Cover and set aside.

2. Heat oil in heavy skillet over medium heat. Add mustard seeds, cover with a lid to avoid splattering and cook for a few seconds until the mustard seeds stop popping. Add chopped onions, ginger and garlic. Fry until onions are golden brown.

3. Drain the marinade into the skillet (don't add shrimp the yet). Add tomatoes and cook for 3–5 minutes. Add jaggery or brown sugar and stir.
4. Add the shrimp and cook for another 3–5 minutes until shrimp transparent and firm to the touch. Add chopped coriander and transfer to a serving platter.

Makes 6 servings (3 cups)   *Exchanges: 1 medium fat meat*
Serving size: ½ cup   *1 vegetable*
Amount per serving:

Calories 107	Carbohydrate . . . . 9 g
Fat . . . . .5 g	Dietary fiber . . . . 2 g
Saturated fat . . . . 0.7 g	Protein . . . . 7 g
Cholesterol . . . . .55 g	Sodium . . . . .430 mg

Jhinga tari
Shrimp in yogurt sauce

If you like shrimp in sauce (curry), you will enjoy this recipe. It is great for special occasions or anytime you want to impress your guests.

1½ lb shrimp, shelled and deveined
¾ tsp salt
2 tbsp vegetable oil
1 medium onion, finely chopped
1 tsp fresh ginger, chopped
2 garlic cloves, chopped
½ tsp cumin powder
¼ tsp turmeric
¼ tsp cayenne pepper (optional)
1 tsp coriander powder
¼ cup plain nonfat yogurt
½ cup water
½ tsp garam masala
1 tsp fresh lemon juice
1 tbsp fresh coriander, finely chopped

1. Season shrimp with ¼ tsp of salt and set aside.
2. Heat oil in a nonstick skillet over medium high heat. Add onions, garlic and ginger. Fry until the onions are golden brown, stirring constantly.
3. Reduce heat to medium. Add turmeric, cayenne pepper and coriander powder. Lightly whip yogurt and add 1 tbsp at a time, stirring constantly. Cook until all the yogurt is absorbed and the mixture draws in to thick mass.
4. Add the shrimp and the remaining ½ tsp salt, stirring to coat the spice mixture evenly. Pour the water evenly over the shrimp. Bring to a boil. Reduce heat to low. Cover tightly and simmer for 8–10 minutes. Shrimp should be firm to the touch. Sprinkle with garam masala and stir lightly.

5. Transfer to a serving platter. Sprinkle with lemon juice and garnish with chopped coriander.

Makes 4 servings (3 cups)   *Exchanges: 1½ medium fat meat*
Serving size: ½ cup
Amount per serving:

Calories	94	Carbohydrate	2 g
Fat	.5 g	Dietary fiber	0.3 g
Saturated fat	0.7 g	Protein	10 g
Cholesterol	83 g	Sodium	369 mg

Meat

I have chosen to include only lamb recipes in this section of this book. Hindus typically do not eat beef and Muslims do not eat pork. If desired, however, most of the lamb recipes can be substituted with beef and some with pork.

Lamb can be very high in fat. For lean cuts, use the leg of lamb for most of the dishes. Trim all the fat and chop or grind the meat. Lamb, beef or pork can all be easily incorporated into a healthy low fat meal plan. The key is to select lean cuts, trim all visible fat and prepare them with low fat cooking methods. In India bones are left in most of the lamb dishes as bones enhance the flavor of the sauce (curry). However, I find boneless lamb much easier to cook and serve. For convenience, I almost always have the butcher trim and chop or grind the meat to my specifications.

Traditionally, lamb is first roasted in oil (bhuna) before it is added to the fried spice mixture (masala) and cooked or simmered to make the sauce (curry). A fair amount of oil may be floating on top of the curry. I have used as little oil as possible to maintain the bhuna flavor, texture and taste. The recipes here are much lower in fat than the traditional ones. Meat, poultry and fish are often cooked with vegetables. The vegetables not only act as a meat extender but also add their own unique flavors to the sauce. They also absorb the flavor of the meat and together they make a great combination.

For nutritional analysis, trimmed leg of lamb was used. The exchanges have been computed to the closest calories possible.

Seekh kebabs
Barbecued lamb on skewers

Seekh (skewer) kebabs are usually barbecued on a grill, but they can be baked in the oven. Serve with coriander chutney, they can be served as an appetizer or part of a meal. Substitute lean beef, if desired.

1 medium onion
1 inch fresh ginger
2 garlic cloves
1 tsp salt
¼ tsp cayenne pepper (optional)
½ tsp coriander powder
½ tsp cumin powder
¾ tsp garam masala
1 lb lean ground lamb

1. In a blender jar grind onions, ginger and garlic. Mix in salt, cayenne pepper, coriander powder, cumin powder and garam masala.
2. In a bowl, mix the lamb and onion mixture thoroughly. Let stand for 20–30 minutes.
3. Preheat oven to broil or prepare the grill.
4. Divide the mixture into 6 equal portions. Lightly oil the skewers. Shape the lamb mixture into sausage shapes on the lightly oiled skewers, about 1 inch thick, gently pressing all around.
5. Barbecue on the grill or broil in the oven for 10–12 minutes on each side, or until well done.

Makes 6 skewers
Serving size: ⅙ recipe
Amount per serving:

Exchanges: 2 medium fat meat

Calories	135	Carbohydrate	1 g
Fat	7 g	Dietary fiber	0 g
Saturated fat	2 g	Protein	16 g
Cholesterol	50 g	Sodium	306 mg

Gosht Kalia

Chopped spicy lamb

Gosht Kalia makes any dinner an elegant event. The roasted almonds add extra crunch and give the dish a festive look. Substitute lean chopped beef or pork, if desired.

1 large onion, finely chopped

1 garlic clove, chopped

1 tbsp fresh ginger, chopped

1 green chili, chopped (optional)

2 lb lean boneless lamb, cut into 1-inch cubes

2 tbsp oil

4 cloves

4 cardamom pods

1 2-inch cinnamon stick

1 tsp cumin powder

1 tbsp coriander powder

1 tsp salt

⅓ cup water

2 tbsp lemon juice

2 tbsp roasted, slivered almonds

1. In a blender grind onion, garlic, ginger and green chili. Set aside.
2. In a heavy skillet cook chopped lamb until meat turns brown. Transfer meat to a bowl and set aside, discarding any fat.
3. In the same pan heat the oil. Add cloves, cardamom, cinnamon stick, cumin and coriander powder and cook for a few seconds. Then add the onion mixture and cook until light brown.
4. Add the meat and salt, stirring to coat with the spices. Add water, stir and bring to a boil. Cover, reduce heat and simmer for 20–30 minutes. Meat should be tender to the touch.

5. Check the sauce. It should be fairly thick. If there is excess liquid, increase the heat to evaporate it. Remove from heat.

6. Add lemon juice and stir. Transfer to a serving dish and garnish with almonds before serving.

Makes 8 servings
Serving size: ⅛ recipe
Amount per serving:

Calories	197	*Exchanges: 3 medium fat meat*	
Fat	10 g	Carbohydrate	2 g
Saturated fat	2.7 g	Dietary fiber	0.5 g
Cholesterol	70 g	Protein	23 g
		Sodium	320 mg

Rogan josh

Lamb in yogurt sauce

This dish originates from the state of Kashmir. It does not use any onions or garlic and has a well blended flavor. The paprika adds a red color to this dish. If desired, you can increase the amount of paprika to enhance the color.

1½ lb lean boneless lamb, cut into 1-inch pieces
1 cup plain nonfat yogurt
2 tsp fresh ginger, chopped
½ tsp ground black pepper
½ tsp turmeric
½ tsp cayenne pepper (optional)
1 tsp salt
1 cup water
2 tbsp fresh coriander, chopped
1 tsp paprika
½ tsp garam masala
pinch of nutmeg

1. Place the lamb in a bowl. In a separate bowl combine yogurt, chopped ginger, black pepper, turmeric, cayenne pepper and salt, mixing well. Pour over the lamb, turning the pieces with a large spoon to coat with the spices. Cover and marinate at room temperature for about 1 hour or in refrigerator for 2 hours or more.
2. Place the lamb and its marinade in a heavy skillet and cook over high heat. Bring to a boil, stirring the meat constantly. Reduce the heat to low, cover the skillet tightly and simmer undisturbed for 30–40 minutes.
3. Pour 1 cup of water down the sides of the pan and sprinkle with chopped coriander and paprika. Stir gently. Cover and simmer for 15–30 minutes or until lamb is tender. Cover and let stand until ready to serve.
4. Transfer to a serving platter and sprinkle the top with garam masala and nutmeg before serving.

Makes 6 servings
Serving size: 1/6 recipe
Amount per serving:
Calories 175
Fat . . . . 6 g
Saturated fat . . . . 2.3 g
Cholesterol . . . . 72 g

Exchanges: 3 lean meat

Carbohydrate . . . . 3 g
Dietary fiber . . . . 0 g
Protein . . . . 25 g
Sodium . . . . .439 mg

Kheema

Ground lamb with peas

This is one of the most-common ways to serve lamb. It tastes great served hot or cold. Substitute lean ground beef if desired. Ground lamb is often very high in fat; for leaner, meat have the butcher grind a trimmed leg of lamb.

1½ lb lean ground lamb
1 tbsp vegetable oil
1 medium onion, finely chopped
4 garlic cloves, chopped
1 tsp fresh ginger, chopped
1 tsp cumin powder
1 tsp coriander powder
¼ tsp cayenne pepper (optional)
1 green chili, finely chopped (optional)
1¼ cup water
¾ cup fresh or frozen peas
4 tbsp chopped fresh coriander (cilantro)
1 tsp salt
1 tsp garam masala
1 tbsp lemon juice

1. Heat a heavy skillet over medium heat, add meat and cook until brown. With a slotted spoon take out the meat and set aside, discarding any fat that cooked out of the meat.
2. In the same pan heat oil. Add onions, garlic and ginger and cook until onions are light brown.
3. Add meat cumin powder, coriander powder, cayenne pepper and chopped green chili. Stir.
4. Add ¾ cup water and bring to a boil. Cover, reduce heat and simmer for 20 minutes, stirring occasionally.

. Add the peas, 2 tbsp of fresh coriander, salt, garam masala, lemon juice and the remaining water. Mix and simmer for another 15 minutes. All the liquid should be absorbed, but if not, open the lid and cook for another few minutes to evaporate it.

. Transfer to a serving dish and garnish with remaining coriander.

Makes 6 servings
Serving size: ⅙ recipe
Amount per serving:

Calories 187
Fat . . . . 8 g
Saturated fat . . . . 2.4 g
Cholesterol . . . . 67 g

Exchanges: 3 lean meat
1 vegetable

Carbohydrate . . . . 4 g
Dietary fiber . . . . 1 g
Protein . . . . 23 g
Sodium . . . . 425 mg

Madrasi gosh
Chopped lamb

As the name suggests this is from the state of Madras. The mustard seeds and the curry leaves lend a very distinct flavor to this dish. You may substitute lean chopped beef or pork, if desired.

2 lb lean boneless lamb, cut into ½-inch pieces
1 tsp salt
2 tsp coriander powder
1 tsp cumin seed powder
¼ tsp cayenne pepper (optional)
2 tsp ground black pepper
2 tbsp vegetable oil
1 tsp mustard seeds
10 curry leaves
1 large onion, thinly sliced
1 tsp fresh ginger, chopped
1½ cups water
1 tbsp lemon juice
2 tbsp fresh coriander, finely chopped (optional)

1. In a large bowl place the lamb and sprinkle with salt, coriander powder, cumin powder, cayenne pepper and black pepper. Stir well to coat with the spices. Let stand at room temperature for about ½ hour.
2. Heat oil in a heavy skillet over medium heat. Add the mustard seeds and cover with a lid to avoid splattering. Add curry leaves, sliced onions and grated ginger. Cook until the onions are lightly brown.
3. Add the lamb and its marinade, stir for about 5 minutes, mixing in all the spices and onions. Stir in the water and bring to a boil. Cover with a lid, reduce heat and simmer undisturbed for 30–45 minutes. The lamb should be tender when pierced with a knife.
4. The sauce should be thick, if necessary, increase the heat and continue to cook until the sauce thickens.

5. Sprinkle with lemon juice and chopped coriander. Stir gently. Serve immediately or cover and let stand until ready to serve. Transfer to a serving platter and serve hot.

Makes 8 servings
Serving size: ⅛ recipe
Amount per serving:

Calories 185		Carbohydrate . . . . 1 g
Fat . . . . 9 g		Dietary fiber . . . . 0 g
Saturated fat . . . . 2.5 g		Protein . . . . 22 g
Cholesterol . . . . .69 g		Sodium . . . . .320 mg

Exchanges: 3 lean meat

Alu gosht
Lamb with potatoes

In India meat is often combined with potatoes. The potatoes absorb the flavor of the meat and the two taste great together. Serve with rice and salad for a complete meal. Substitute lean chopped beef or pork, if desired.

1½ lb lean boneless lamb, cut into 1-inch pieces
1 tbsp vegetable oil
1 medium onion, thinly sliced
2 garlic cloves, chopped
1 tbsp fresh ginger, chopped
1 tsp cumin powder
½ tsp turmeric
½ tsp cayenne pepper (optional)
3 medium tomatoes, cut into 1-inch pieces
or 1 can (16 oz) chopped tomatoes
3 medium potatoes, peeled and cut into 1½-inch pieces
1½ tsp salt
3 cups water
2 tbsp fresh coriander, finely chopped

1. In a heavy skillet cook chopped lamb until meat turns brown. Transfer meat to a bowl and set aside. Discard any fat that cooked out of the meat.
2. Heat oil in the same skillet over medium high heat. Add sliced onions, garlic and ginger. Fry until the onions turn light brown. Add the lamb, cumin powder, turmeric and cayenne pepper.
3. Add chopped tomatoes, potatoes and salt. Stir and cook for 5 minutes, completely blending in all the spices. Add water and bring to a boil. Cover with a lid, reduce heat and simmer undisturbed for about 30–45 minutes until the meat is tender.

. Sprinkle with chopped coriander and stir. The sauce should be thick so, if necessary, increase the heat and cook to desired consistency.

Makes 6 servings
Serving size: ⅙ recipe
Amount per serving:

Calories	244	
Fat	.8 g	
Saturated fat	2.4 g	
Cholesterol	.67 g	

Exchanges: 3 lean meat
1 starch

Carbohydrate	18 g
Dietary fiber	2 g
Protein	23 g
Sodium	.594 mg

Koftas
Lamb meatballs

Koftas are made with a variety of meat and vegetables. Koftas are usually deep-fat fried and then cooked in a sauce. I usually bake my meat koftas and then add them to a low fat sauce. For best results, cook this dish a few hours before serving so that the meatballs will absorb the flavor of the sauce. Substitute lean ground beef, if desired.

1 lb lean ground lamb

1 egg

1 tsp salt

2 medium onions

1 inch fresh ginger, chopped

4 garlic cloves

1 green chili (optional)

2 tbsp vegetable oil

½ tsp cumin seeds

½-inch cinnamon stick

½ tsp turmeric

1 tsp coriander powder

1 tsp ground black pepper

½ cup plain yogurt

1½ cup water

1½ tsp garam masala

1. Preheat oven to 450° F.
2. In a bowl put lamb, egg and ½ tsp of salt and mix well. Wetting your hands with cold water to keep the meat from sticking, make balls about 1½ inches round, packing firmly.
3. Place meatballs in a single layer in a lightly oiled baking dish. Bake for 18–20 minutes until meat is no longer pink.

4. Remove from the oven, discarding any fat and transfer to a shallow baking dish. Reduce oven to 300° F.

5. In the meantime grind the onions, ginger, garlic and green chili in a blender. Set aside.

6. Heat oil in a heavy skillet over medium heat. Add the cumin seeds and cinnamon stick. Fry for a few seconds until cumin seeds are golden brown. Add the onion paste. Fry until light brown.

7. Whip yogurt with a wire wisk and add 1 tbsp at a time to the onions, stirring constantly. Add turmeric, coriander powder, black pepper and the remaining ½ tsp of salt. Continue to fry until the mixture is thick and draws into a dense mass. Add water and bring to a boil, simmering for 5 minutes.

8. Pour sauce over the meatballs and sprinkle with garam masala. Cover with aluminum foil and bake at 300° F for 15–20 minutes. Serve immediately or cover and let sit until ready to serve.

Makes 6 servings
Serving size: ⅙ recipe
Amount per serving:

Exchanges: 2 ½ medium fat
meat

Calories 172	Carbohydrate . . . . 4 g
Fat . . . . 10 g	Dietary fiber . . . . 0 g
Saturated fat . . . . 2.3 g	Protein . . . . 17 g
Cholesterol . . . . 82 g	Sodium . . . . 416 mg

Boti kebabs

Lamb kebabs

Lamb kebabs are very popular and help make any party a great success. The marinated lamb can be barbecued on the grill or baked in the oven. Substitute lean chopped beef, if desired.

1 lb lean boneless lamb, cut into 1–2-inch cubes
⅓ cup plain nonfat yogurt
1 tbsp fresh ginger, chopped
2 garlic cloves, chopped
¼ tsp cayenne pepper
1 tsp coriander powder
¾ tsp salt
½ tsp garam masala

1. Parboil lamb pieces for 10–15 minutes. Discard any juices. Pat dry with paper towels and place in a mixing bowl.
2. Mix yogurt, ginger, garlic, cayenne pepper, coriander powder, salt and garam masala. Add to the lamb pieces and stir to coat with the spices. Marinate for 2 hours at room temperature or overnight in the refrigerator.
3. Preheat oven to broil or prepare the grill.
4. Thread 5–6 pieces on each lightly oiled skewer, leaving a little gap between each piece. Brush on the marinade.
5. Cook the kebabs under the broiler or on the grill. In the oven, broil for 10 minutes on each side or until tender. Brush with remaining marinade to prevent drying. Do not overcook. Serve hot.

Makes 6 servings
Serving size: ⅙ recipe
Amount per serving:

Exchanges: 2 lean meat

Calories 107	Carbohydrate . . . . 1 g
Fat .4 g	Dietary fiber . . . . 0 g
Saturated fat . . . . 1.4 g	Protein . . . . 15 g
Cholesterol . . . . .46 g	Sodium . . . . .311 mg

Yogurt, salads and chutneys

Yogurt is an essential part of many Indian meals. Plain yogurt is eaten all over India. It is served plain or as raita which is yogurt combined with variety of vegetables or occasionally with sugar and fruit. Yogurt is mostly eaten with a dash of salt, which is such a great contrast to the sweetened yogurt eaten in the Western World. Plain yogurt often accompanies a meal as a side dish; it is soothing and cooling with a spicy meal. In south India, a meal is invariably topped off with rice and plain yogurt. Nutritionally speaking, yogurt combined with grains also provides the amino acids to make complete protein.

Salads are often served with a meal for crunch and variety. Favorite ingredients are cucumbers, tomatoes, onions and radishes. Lettuce is not as popular in India as in the Western World, although it is catching on. Salads are more often served as a relish than as a meal or a side dish.

Chutneys and pickles are condiments that are served with meals. They come in salty, sour, sweet or hot flavors. The pickles are very potent and only a dab is needed to perk up any meal. Pickles are usually made in huge jars and kept for one year or longer. Many chutneys are made fresh daily but can be kept for a few days in the refrigerator. I sometimes freeze chutneys for later use. A little bit of chutney adds a lot of flavor.

Dahi

Plain yogurt

Homemade yogurt is easy to prepare and tastes better than store-bought. Since I use a fair amount of yogurt, I prepare 4–6 cups at a time. It will keep in the refrigerator for up to 10 days. The secret is to refrigerate it as soon as it is set, otherwise, it becomes too sour. The homemade yogurt has more liquid whereas store-bought yogurt has gelatin or pectin to make it set more firmly. For culture, use only plain yogurt with active culture. Once you get the yogurt to set, use that yogurt for culture. It will improve with age. Even if you don't plan to make yogurt on a regular basis, you can keep about 2 tablespoons of yogurt for culture in a air-tight container for days.

4 cups skim milk
¼ cup nonfat dry milk
2 tsp low fat plain yogurt (plain yogurt with active culture)

1. Mix skim milk and nonfat dry milk. Bring to a full boil. Stir frequently to avoid burning at the bottom. I usually boil milk in the microwave for convenience. Cool milk until lukewarm (about 110°F). It should be warm to the touch. I usually check it with my (washed) finger. Add culture to the milk and stir thoroughly.
2. Cover with a lid and keep in a warm place for 6–10 hours or overnight until it is set. (I usually keep it in the oven, and in the winter I turn the oven light on to keep it warm.) Refrigerate for 2 hours or longer and serve cold.

Makes 4 servings (4 cups)
Serving size:1 cup
Amount per serving:

Calories 100		Carbohydrate . . . . 14 g	
Fat .0 g		Dietary fiber . . . . 0 g	
Saturated fat . . . . .0 g		Protein . . . . 10 g	
Cholesterol . . . . .5 g		Sodium . . . . .150 mg	

Exchange: 1 milk

Kheere ka raita

Yogurt with cucumber

To make a nice accompaniment to any meal, serve this cool and refreshing combination of yogurt and cucumber.

2 cups plain nonfat yogurt
1½ cups cucumber, peeled and grated
½ tsp salt
½ tsp roasted cumin seed powder*
¼ tsp cayenne pepper (optional)

1. Stir yogurt with a wire wisk in a small serving bowl.
2. Gently squeeze grated cucumber by hand to remove the excess liquid. Add to the yogurt. Add salt and stir.
3. Garnish with roasted cumin seed powder and cayenne pepper. Do not stir. Serve immediately or cover and refrigerate until ready to serve.

Makes 6 servings (3 cups)
Serving size: ½ cup
Amount per serving:

Calories 50		Carbohydrate . . . . 7 g	
Fat .0 g		Dietary fiber . . . . .0.5 g	
Saturated fat . . . . .0 g		Protein . . . . 5 g	
Cholesterol . . . . .1 g		Sodium . . . . .237 mg	

Exchanges: ½ milk
1 vegetable

---

* See recipe Roasted cumin powder on page 54.

Tamatar piaz ka raita
Yogurt with tomatoes and onion

Serve this raita as a salad or an accompaniment to any meal.

2 cups nonfat plain yogurt
1 cup tomato, chopped into ¼-inch cubes
½ cup cucumber, chopped into ¼-inch cubes
½ cup onion, finely chopped
¾ tsp salt
½ tsp roasted cumin seed powder*
¼ tsp cayenne pepper (optional)

1. Stir yogurt with wire wisk in a small serving bowl.
2. Add chopped tomatoes, cucumber, onion and salt. Stir.
3. Garnish with roasted cumin seed powder and cayenne pepper. Serve immediately or cover and refrigerate until ready to serve.

Makes 8 servings (4 cups)
Serving size: ½ cup
Amount per serving:

		Exchanges: ½ milk	
		1 vegetable	
Calories	40	Carbohydrate	6 g
Fat	0 g	Dietary fiber	0.5 g
Saturated fat	0 g	Protein	4 g
Cholesterol	1 g	Sodium	245 mg

---

* See recipe Roasted cumin powder on page 54.

Alu ka raita

Yogurt with potatoes

If you like potatoes, try this combination.

2 small potatoes, boiled
2 cups nonfat plain yogurt
¾ tsp salt
½ tsp roasted cumin seed powder*
¼ tsp cayenne pepper (optional)

1. Peel boiled and cooled potatoes. Cut into ½-inch pieces. Set aside.
2. In a bowl mix yogurt and salt with a wire wisk. Add potato pieces and stir.
3. Garnish with cumin seed powder and cayenne pepper. Do not stir in. Serve immediately or cover and refrigerate until ready to serve.

Makes 6 servings (3 cups)
Serving size: ½ cup
Amount per serving:

Exchanges: ½ milk
½ starch

Calories 72	Carbohydrate . . . . 13 g
Fat . . . . .0 g	Dietary fiber . . . . .0.4 g
Saturated fat . . . . .0 g	Protein . . . . 5 g
Cholesterol . . . . .1 g	Sodium . . . . .326 mg

---

*   See recipe Roasted cumin powder on page 54.

Kele ka raita
Yogurt with banana

Kele ka raita makes a great side dish or a light dessert. My children eat it like pudding.

2 cups nonfat plain yogurt
3 tbsp sugar
2 ripe bananas

1. Mix yogurt and sugar with a wire whip.
2. Peel and slice bananas into ¼-inch circles. Add to yogurt and stir gently.
3. Serve immediately or cover and refrigerate until ready to serve.

Makes 6 servings (3 cups)
Serving size: ½ cup
Amount per serving:

Calories 100		Carbohydrate . . . . 21 g
Fat . . . . 0 g		Dietary fiber . . . . 0.6 g
Saturated fat . . . . 0 g		Protein . . . . 5 g
Cholesterol . . . . 1 g		Sodium . . . . 58 mg

Exchanges: ½ milk
1 fruit

Piaz aur tamatar ka salad

Onion and tomato salad

This salad is easy to prepare and is a colorful addition to any meal.

1 medium red onion, sliced into ¼-inch wedges
2 tbsp lemon juice
¾ tsp salt
2 medium tomatoes, sliced into ¼-inch wedges
½ tsp ground black pepper

1. Combine onion wedges, lemon juice and ½ tsp of salt. Cover and marinate for 20 minutes or longer. Stir occasionally. Drain and discard the juice.
2. Add tomato wedges and sprinkle with remaining ¼ tsp salt and black pepper. Toss lightly to mix.
3. Serve immediately or cover and refrigerate until ready to serve.

Makes 6 servings
Serving size: ⅙ recipe
Amount per serving:

Exchange: 1 vegetable

Calories	17	Carbohydrate	4 g
Fat	0 g	Dietary fiber	1 g
Saturated fat	0 g	Protein	1 g
Cholesterol	0 g	Sodium	182 mg

Cachumber

Tomato, cucumber, onion salad

This low fat salad tastes great with any meal.

2 cups tomatoes, finely chopped
1 cup cucumber, finely chopped
½ cup onion, finely chopped
¼ cup fresh coriander, finely chopped
½ tsp salt
1 tbsp fresh lemon juice
½ tsp roasted cumin seed powder*

1. In a serving bowl, mix tomatoes, cucumbers, onions, coriander, salt and lemon juice. Toss gently. sprinkle with cumin seed powder.
2. Serve immediately or cover and refrigerate until ready to serve.

Makes 6 servings (3 cups)   *Exchange: 1 vegetable*
Serving size: ½ cup
Amount per serving:
Calories 20   Carbohydrate . . . . 4 g
Fat . . . . 0 g   Dietary fiber . . . . 1.4 g
Saturated fat . . . . 0 g   Protein . . . . 1 g
Cholesterol . . . . 0 g   Sodium . . . . 182 mg

---

* See recipe Roasted cumin powder on page 54.

Chana-rajmah salad
Mixed bean salad

Canned beans are used for this easy bean salad recipe. It keeps in refrigerator for up to a week and is good for brown bag lunches.

1 lb can chickpeas
1 lb can black-eyed peas
1 lb can red kidney beans
1 garlic clove, crushed
2 tbsp olive oil
½ cup finely chopped green onions
  including 1 inch of the green tops
3 tbsp chopped fresh coriander (cilantro)
1 green chili, seeded and finely chopped
¼ tsp roasted cumin seed powder*
⅛ tsp fresh ground black pepper
½ tsp salt
3 tbsp fresh lemon juice

1. Drain chickpeas, black-eyed peas and kidney beans in a colander. Rinse with cold water. Pat dry with paper towels. Set aside.
2. Combine olive oil and garlic in a small bowl. Set aside.
3. Mix onions, coriander, green chili, cumin powder, black pepper, salt and lemon juice in a large salad bowl.
4. Add the beans and oil with garlic.
5. Toss thoroughly. Cover with plastic wrap and refrigerate for 2 hours or longer.

---

* See recipe Roasted cumin powder on page 54.

Makes 12 servings (6 cups)
Serving size: ½ cup
Amount per serving:
Calories 115
Fat . . . . 3 g
Saturated fat . . . . 0 g
Cholesterol . . . . 0 g

Exchanges: 1 starch
1 lean meat

Carbohydrate . . . . 16 g
Dietary fiber . . . . 5 g
Protein . . . . 6 g
Sodium . . . . 150 mg

Gobhi-gajar salad
Cabbage and carrot salad

Serve this salad as a side dish with any Indian or Western meal. It is cooked to just the right tenderness and is mildly spiced.

4 cups cabbage, thinly sliced
1 cup carrots, peeled and grated
1 tsp vegetable oil
½ tsp mustard seeds
pinch of turmeric
½ tsp salt
¼ tsp black pepper

1. Wash and prepare the cabbage and carrots. Set aside.
2. Heat oil in a heavy skillet on high heat. Add mustard seeds, cover with a lid to avoid splattering and cook for a few seconds until the mustard seeds stop popping. Add the cabbage and carrots and then the turmeric, salt and pepper. Stir to mix. Stir-fry for 3–4 minutes, until heated through. Do not overcook. The cabbage should be just barely cooked.
3. Transfer to a serving platter immediately.

Makes 4 servings (2 cups)
Serving size: ½ cup
Amount per serving:

Exchange: 1 vegetable

Calories	38	Carbohydrate	6 g
Fat	1 g	Dietary fiber	2.4 g
Saturated fat	0 g	Protein	1 g
Cholesterol	0 g	Sodium	288 mg

Muli lachha

Radish salad

For radish lovers, this is a nice change from the ordinary. It is usually served in the winter in India, when fresh, tender, white, long radishes are abundant.

2 cups grated fresh white radishes (Dakins)
¼ tsp salt
2 tbsp lemon juice

1. Squeeze excess water from the grated radishes between the palms of your hands.
2. In a salad bowl mix squeezed radishes, salt and lemon juice. Toss thoroughly. Cover and marinate in the refrigerator for 20–30 minutes.

Makes 4 servings (2 cups)
Serving size: ½ cup
Amount per serving:

Exchange: free vegetable

Calories	6	Carbohydrate	1 g
Fat	0 g	Dietary fiber	1 g
Saturated fat	0 g	Protein	0 g
Cholesterol	0 g	Sodium	138 mg

Phul gobhi salad

Stir-fried salad

Serve this salad for a colorful and refreshing accompaniment to any Indian or Western meal.

½ medium cauliflower, cut into small florets
1 medium bell pepper, sliced
1 medium red pepper, sliced
1 small zucchini, sliced into strips
4 carrots, sliced
2 tsp vegetable oil
¾ tsp salt
½–1 tsp black pepper

1. Wash and prepare all the vegetables. Set aside.
2. Heat oil in a heavy skillet or a wok on high heat. Add all the vegetables, salt and pepper. Stir-fry for 5–7 minutes until heated through. Vegetables should be tender but intact. Do not overcook the vegetables.
3. Remove from the heat and transfer to a serving dish immediately.

Makes 6 servings (4 cups)
Serving size: ¾ cup
Amount per serving:

Calories	33	Carbohydrate	5 g
Fat	1 g	Dietary fiber	1.9 g
Saturated fat	0 g	Protein	1 g
Cholesterol	0 g	Sodium	214 mg

Exchange: 1 vegetable

Kabuli chana salad

Marinated chickpea salad

This light salad is great with a sandwich or pulao. Marinating gives chickpeas a real zip.

2 (16 oz) cans chickpeas
4 carrots, diced
½ cup green onions, chopped
¼ tsp salt
½ tsp black pepper, coarsely ground
2 tbsp lemon juice
2 tbsp chopped fresh coriander

1. Drain chickpeas in a strainer and rinse with cold running water. Pat dry. Place in a salad bowl.
2. Add the diced carrots and chopped green onions. Mix well. Sprinkle with salt, black pepper, lemon juice and the chopped coriander, tossing to mix well. Refrigerate for 1 hour or longer.

Makes 8 servings (4 cups)
Serving size: ½ cup
Amount per serving:

Exchanges: 1 starch
1 lean meat

Calories 110	Carbohydrate . . . . 19 g
Fat . . . . 1.5 g	Dietary fiber . . . . 6 g
Saturated fat . . . . 0 g	Protein . . . . 5 g
Cholesterol . . . . 0 g	Sodium . . . . 180 mg

Aam ka laccha
Mango salad

In season, the sweet-and-sour taste of an underripe mango when combined with salt and cayenne pepper adds an excellent taste to any meal. It is eaten more like a pickle, in a small quantity, rather than like a salad.

1 firm, underripe mango (¾ lb)
⅛–¼ tsp cayenne pepper
½ tsp salt

1. Wash and peel mango. Slice mango flesh into 1-inch strips. Discard the mango seed.
2. Toss mango slices with cayenne pepper and salt in a mixing bowl. Cover and marinate for 30 minutes or longer in the refrigerator.
3. Serve cold or refrigerate for up to 2–3 days.

Makes 16 servings (2 cups) *Exchanges: free*
Serving size: 2 tbsp
Amount per serving:

Calories	12	Carbohydrate	3 g
Fat	0 g	Dietary fiber	0.5 g
Saturated fat	0 g	Protein	0 g
Cholesterol	0 g	Sodium	67 mg

Dhania chutney
Coriander chutney

The bright green color and the hot and sour taste of dhania chutney adds a zip to any dish. It is the most-popular chutney served with meals or snacks. It is eaten with just about anything—pulao, samosas, dal and chapati or chicken and rice. It keeps well in the refrigerator for up to two weeks, although the color might change to dark green. I often freeze the extra to retain its bright green color.

1 small bunch (3½–4 oz) fresh coriander (cilantro)
¼ cup onion, coarsely chopped
½ tsp cumin seeds
1–2 green chilies
1 tsp salt
3 tbsp lemon juice

1. Clean coriander of any discolored leaves and stems. Cut about 1 inch from the tips of the stems. Leave the rest of the stems intact. It is often full of sand so wash thoroughly in 2–3 changes of water.
2. Place onion, cumin seeds, green chilies, salt, lemon juice and coriander in a blender jar and grind to a smooth paste.
3. Serve immediately or cover and refrigerate until ready to serve.

Makes about 1 cup
Serving size: 1 tsp
Amount per serving:

Exchanges: free

Calories 1	Carbohydrate 0
Fat . . . . .0 g	Dietary fiber . . . . 0 g
Saturated fat . . . . .0 g	Protein . . . . 0 g
Cholesterol . . . . .0 g	Sodium . . . . .44 mg

Pudina chutney
Mint Chutney

The refreshing flavor of this sweet-and-sour chutney is a nice accompaniment to any meal.

2 cups fresh mint leaves (about 1 oz), cleaned and washed
⅛ tsp cumin seeds
1 green chili, chopped
¾ tsp salt
2 tbsp lemon juice
2 tbsp sugar

1. In a blender jar combine all the ingredients and grind to a smooth paste.
2. Transfer to a serving dish, serve immediately or cover and refrigerate until ready to serve. The chutney can be kept in the refrigerator for 1–2 weeks. It may change color over time, but the taste is unaltered. It can be frozen for later use. Freezing also retains the color.

Makes about ½ cup
Serving size: 1 tsp
Amount per serving:

Exchange: free

Calories 4	Carbohydrate 1
Fat . . . . 0 g	Dietary fiber . . . . 0 g
Saturated fat . . . . 0 g	Protein . . . . 0 g
Cholesterol . . . . 0 g	Sodium . . . . 66 mg

Imli chutney

Tamarind chutney

Tamarind has a unique sweet-sour taste. This delicious chutney can be used as a condiment with several things. It is made in many different ways. I like to cook mine as it gives it a smoother taste and also keeps for a much longer time— about a month in the refrigerator. And it can also be frozen for later use.

½ pack (3½ oz) dry tamarind
3 cups water
1½ tsp salt
¾ cup brown sugar
½ tsp cayenne pepper

1. Remove any seeds from the tamarind. Combine tamarind and 2 cups of water in a medium pan, bring to a boil and cook for 2–3 minutes. Remove from the heat. Let soak for ½–1 hour.
2. Grind the soaked tamarind in a blender. Strain the pulp in the strainer. Pour the remaining water (1 cup) over the pulp gradually, stirring with a spoon or fingers to help strain the tamarind paste.
3. Return the tamarind paste to the pan. Add the salt, brown sugar and cayenne pepper. Stir until the sugar is dissolved. Heat on medium heat, stirring occasionally. Bring to a boil, reduce heat and simmer for 15–20 minutes. The chutney will thicken as it cools.
4. Serve at room temperature or refrigerate in an air-tight container.

Makes about 2¼ cups
Serving size: 1 tsp
Amount per serving:

Exchange: free

Calories 14	Carbohydrate . . . . 4 g
Fat . . . . .0 g	Dietary fiber . . . . 0 g
Saturated fat . . . . .0 g	Protein . . . . 0 g
Cholesterol . . . . .0 g	Sodium . . . . .55 mg

Tamatar chutney
Tomato chutney

I often make tomato chutney during the summer when tomatoes are abundant and inexpensive. I also freeze some for later use. Serve this chutney with any dal or meat dish.

4 medium firm, ripe tomatoes (about 1½ lb)
1 tsp vegetable oil
¼ tsp mustard seeds
¼ tsp kalonji (onion seeds)
1 tsp salt
1 green chili, seeded and chopped (optional)
1 tsp coriander powder
2 tbsp sugar

1. Wash, core and coarsely chop tomatoes. Set aside.
2. In a medium pan heat oil over medium heat. Add mustard seeds and cover with a lid to avoid splattering. Cook for few seconds until the seed stop popping. Add chopped tomatoes, kalonji, salt, chopped green chili and coriander powder. Cover with a lid and simmer for 15–20 minutes. Stir occasionally.
3. Remove the lid and cook for another 10–15 minutes, stirring occasionally until the chutney is of desired consistency. Stir in sugar.
4. Transfer to a serving dish or store in air-tight container. The chutney will keep in the refrigerator for 2–3 weeks. It can also be frozen for later use.

Makes about 2 cups
Serving size: 1 tbsp
Amount per serving:

Calories	8	Carbohydrate	1 g
Fat	0 g	Dietary fiber	0 g
Saturated fat	0 g	Protein	0 g
Cholesterol	0 g	Sodium	68 mg

Exchange: free

Nariyal chutney
Coconut chutney

Coconut chutney is very popular in south India where coconuts are abundant. It tastes great with idlies or dhokla.

¼ cup chana dal
1 dry red chili (optional)
½ cup fresh coconut, coarsely chopped
½ tsp salt
½ cup water
¼ cup nonfat yogurt

1. In a small fry pan dry-roast chana dal and red chili over medium heat until the dal turns reddish brown. Remove from the heat and cool.
2. Grind dal, chopped coconut, salt and water in a blender and grind to a smooth paste. Stir in yogurt.
3. Transfer to a serving dish. Serve immediately or cover and refrigerate until ready to use. It can also be frozen for later use.

Makes about 1½ cups *Exchange: free*
Serving size: 1 tbsp
Amount per serving:
Calories 15   Carbohydrate . . . . 2 g
Fat . . . . 0.7 g   Dietary fiber . . . . 0.7 g
Saturated fat . . . . 0.5 g   Protein . . . . 1 g
Cholesterol . . . . 0 g   Sodium . . . . 48 mg

Mungfali chutney
Peanut chutney

From the state of Maharashtra comes this very popular chutney. It is an excellent alternative to peanut butter. Serve with fresh or leftover roti or toast.

½ cup unsalted dry-roasted peanuts
¼ tsp cumin seeds
½ tsp salt
¼ tsp cayenne pepper

1. In a blender (preferably the small jar) grind the peanuts, cumin seeds, salt and cayenne pepper just until the peanuts are ground and bind slightly. Do not grind too long as it will turn into peanut butter.
2. Store in a air-tight container.

Makes 10 servings (⅔ cup)   *Exchange: 1 fat*
Serving size: 1 tbsp
Amount per serving:

Calories	42	Carbohydrate	1 g
Fat	3.5 g	Dietary fiber	0.6 g
Saturated fat	0.5 g	Protein	2 g
Cholesterol	0 g	Sodium	108 mg

Desserts

Indian sweets are very different from the Western ones. The variety of sweets available is endless. Some of the basic categories of sweets are barfi, halwa, laddu and kheer. There are no equivalent Western names. Chocolate is not served as a dessert, but it is available as a candy.

I have included some simple or easy-to-make desserts in this book. Desserts by category are typically high in fat and calories. I have kept the fat down wherever possible. By limiting frequency and quantity of desserts, one can enjoy a variety without compromising health.

Sooji halwa
Cream of wheat halwa

Here is the most-popular halwa throughout India. It is often the choice of sweets offered as prasad (communion) at prayer meetings or at the temples. I grew up eating it for occasional Sunday breakfasts. Use ghee or butter for the special flavor and taste.

½ cup cream of wheat (sooji)
2 tbsp ghee or unsalted butter
2 tbsp blanched slivered almonds
½ cup sugar
2 cups water
1 tbsp golden raisins
4 cardamom pods

1. In a heavy saucepan combine cream of wheat and ghee. Heat over medium low heat, stirring constantly until cream of wheat turns golden brown (about 15 minutes). Add almonds and cook for 1 more minute.
2. Add water, stir and bring to a boil.
3. Stir in sugar. Cover with a lid, leaving a small crack open to allow steam to escape. Reduce heat and simmer for 10–15 minutes or until most of the water is absorbed, stirring occasionally. (Stir carefully to avoid burning as the halwa tends to splatter.)
4. Add raisins and stir. Transfer to a serving dish.
5. Remove seeds from cardamom pods and crush with a mortar and pestle. Garnish the halwa with the cardamom powder.

Makes 6 servings (3 cups)
Serving size: ½ cup
Amount per serving:
Calories 160
Fat . . . . .5 g
Saturated fat . . . . 2.5 g
Cholesterol . . . . 10 g

Exchanges: 2 starches
1 fat
Carbohydrate . . . . 28 g
Dietary fiber . . . . 1 g
Protein . . . . 2 g
Sodium . . . . .2 mg

Kheer

Rice pudding

Kheer is often referred to as rice pudding and is probably the most-popular pudding in India. It does not taste anything like the Western rice pudding. It has a delicate, mild flavor. Traditionally it is made with whole milk and cream, but here is a lower fat version. You will not miss the fat in this recipe. Although it can be made with skim milk, for best results, use low fat milk.

½ gallon low fat milk
¼ cup basmati rice, washed
⅓ cup sugar
4 cardamom pods
2 tbsp slivered almonds
2 tbsp golden raisins

1. In a large, heavy saucepan, heat milk over medium heat. Stir frequently to avoid sticking at the bottom of the pan. Add washed rice and bring to a boil. Reduce heat and simmer for 1–1½ hours on low heat. Stir occasionally to make sure the pudding does not stick to the bottom.
2. When pudding is the right consistency (about ⅔–½ of the original amount), remove from the heat. Kheer will thicken as it cools.
3. Remove the cardamom seeds from the pods and crush finely with a mortar and pestle. Add sugar, almonds, raisins and cardamom powder to the pudding. Stir to mix.
4. Transfer to a serving container and cover with a lid. Serve warm or refrigerate and serve chilled.

Makes 8 servings (4 cups)
Serving size: ½ cup

Amount per serving:
Calories 189
Fat . . . . 5.5 g
Saturated fat . . . . .3 g
Cholesterol . . . . .18 g

Exchanges: 1 milk
1 starch
1 fat

Carbohydrate . . . . 26 g
Dietary fiber. . . . . .0.4 g
Protein . . . . 9 g
Sodium . . . . .123 mg

Gajar halwa
Carrot halwa

In India this is a very popular dessert, especially in the winter when carrots are fresh. I still make it in the winter although carrots are available all year. Traditionally it is made with milk and cream and roasted in ghee and is often cooked for hours to get the creamy taste and texture. Here is my quick and lower fat version with all the taste and half the hassle.

2 lb carrots, grated
2 cups skim milk
1 can skim evaporated milk (12 oz)
1 carton part skim ricotta cheese (15 oz)
1 cup sugar
4 cardamom pods
2 tbsp slivered almonds (optional)

1. Place grated carrots and skim milk in a heavy skillet on medium heat. Bring to a boil, reduce heat and simmer for 20 minutes. Stir periodically to avoid burning at the bottom.
2. Add the evaporated skim milk and continue to cook until most of the milk is evaporated.
3. In the meantime in a separate nonstick fry pan, put the ricotta cheese. Cook on medium heat for 8–10 minutes until most of the liquid is evaporated. Stir periodically to avoid burning at the bottom. Do not stir too much. The cheese should become slightly crumbly.
4. Add the ricotta cheese and sugar to the carrots and mix. Continue to simmer, cooking until most of the liquid is evaporated. The halwa should be moist, not dry and crumbly. Remove from the heat.
5. Remove seeds from cardamom pods and crush with a mortar and pestle. Add the crushed seeds to the halwa.

6. Transfer to a serving platter and garnish with almonds. Serve warm or cold.

Makes 8 servings (4 cups)
Serving size: ½ cup

Amount per serving:

Calories 271
Fat . . . . .5 g
Saturated fat . . . . 2.5 g
Cholesterol . . . . .17 g

Exchanges: 2 starches
1 milk
1 fat

Carbohydrate . . . . 46 g
Dietary fiber . . . . .3.4 g
Protein . . . . 12 g
Sodium . . . . .182 mg

Mango ice cream

This recipe is adapted for the ice cream maker. The evaporated milk gives it a rich and creamy taste. This is a lower fat version of the ice cream. For convenience use canned mango pulp.

2 cups half-and-half
1 can (12 oz) evaporated skim milk
½ cup skim milk
1 cup sugar
¾ cup mango pulp
½ tsp mango essence (optional)

1. Mix all the above ingredients in an ice cream maker. Make ice cream according to the ice cream maker's instructions.
2. Serve right away from the ice cream maker or freeze and serve later.

Makes 16 servings (½ gallon)   *Exchanges: 1 starch*
Serving size: ½ cup   *½ fat*
Amount per serving:

Calories	118	Carbohydrate	20 g
Fat	3 g	Dietary fiber	0.4 g
Saturated fat	2 g	Protein	3 g
Cholesterol	12 g	Sodium	44 mg

Nariyal barfi

Coconut sweets

Barfies are typically diamond-shaped sweets. Here is a lower fat version of nariyal barfi that can be whipped up in a jiffy.

1 (15 oz) carton part skim ricotta cheese
1½ cups nonfat dry milk powder
1¾ cups sugar
1½ cups desiccated shredded coconut*

1. Grease an 8 × 8-inch square pan. Set aside.
2. In a large, nonstick fry pan heat ricotta cheese on medium heat. Add milk powder and stir to mix thoroughly. Cook for 12–15 minutes until most of the liquid is evaporated. Stir frequently to avoid sticking or burning on the bottom.
3. Add sugar and stir. The ricotta cheese mixture will become liquid again. Cook for another 5 minutes, stirring occasionally. Add the coconut and mix thoroughly. Continue to cook for 3–5 minutes. The mixture should be quite thick.
4. Pour the mixture into the greased pan and press the mixture with a spatula. Cut into 1 × 1-inch diamond shapes. The mixture sets as it cools. Cool completely before removing from the pan.

Makes about 24 pieces
Serving size: 1 piece (¹/24 recipe)
Amount per serving:

Calories 125		Carbohydrate . . . . 18 g	
Fat . . . . .5 g		Dietary fiber . . . . 0 g	
Saturated fat . . . . .3 g		Protein . . . . 4 g	
Cholesterol . . . . .6 g		Sodium . . . . .44 mg	

Exchanges: 1 starch
1 fat

---

* Use unsweetened very finely shredded coconut. See page 47.

Kaju barfi
Cashew sweets

Cashew barfi is a delicacy. Served at special occasions, they just melt in your mouth. Barfi is often covered with a edible silver foil which gives it an elegant look. The silver foil does not alter the taste in any way.

1 cup raw cashews

1 cup sugar

½ cup water

3–4 silver foils (optional)

1. Using a coffee grinder, grind cashews to a fine powder. (A blender may be used, but it does not grind nuts as finely.) Set aside.
2. In a large skillet place sugar and water. Cook over medium heat, bring to a boil and simmer for about 8–10 minutes until the syrup reaches the soft ball stage. (To test for the soft ball stage, take some water in a small plate and pour a drop of syrup in the water. If the drop of syrup can be picked up with your fingers and rolled into a soft ball, the syrup is ready. If the syrup is too thin you will not be able to pick it up, and if it is too thick the ball will be hard and dry.) Remove from heat.
3. Add cashew powder and mix well. Cool for about 5–10 minutes, mixing occasionally to prevent drying. The cashew mixture will thicken as it cools. The mix should still be warm but cool enough to touch.
4. Mix the cashew mixture thoroughly and pour onto the counter. It will have the consistency of a dough. Mix again and make it into a smooth flat ball.
5. Place flattened ball into the center of a buttered paper. Put another butter paper on top. Using a rolling pin, roll out the dough about ¼ inch thick. Remove the top buttered paper. (If you want to use silver foil, carefully place on the rolled out dough. The silver foil is very delicate and it will stick to the barfi immediately. Once placed it cannot be removed.) Cut into 1-inch diamond shapes. Remove the bottom buttered paper and place the barfies in a single layer on a plate or tray.

6. Allow the barfies to air-dry for about 20–30 minutes before storing in an air-tight container. The barfies can be served immediately, kept at room temperature for up to 2 weeks, refrigerated for a month or frozen for later use.

Makes about 24 pieces
Serving size: 1 barfi
Amount per serving:

		Exchanges: ½ starch	
		½ fat	
Calories	62	Carbohydrate	10 g
Fat	2.5 g	Dietary fiber	0.4 g
Saturated fat	0.5 g	Protein	1 g
Cholesterol	0 g	Sodium	1 mg

Kulfi

Indian ice cream

Kulfi is the original version of the ice cream available in India. It is very popular in the summer in north India. It is sold plain or with phaluda (thin plain noodles). I remember visiting my grandparents in the summer and every afternoon eating kulfi on a stick bought from a vender who would come by yelling "tundi tundi kulfi." This kulfi recipe is quick and lower in fat with the excellent original flavor and taste.

4 cups low fat milk
2 cans (12 oz) evaporated whole milk
1 cup sugar
¼ tsp rose essence (optional)
2 tbsp pistachios, crushed

1. Using a nonstick fry pan, bring low fat milk to a boil over medium high heat, stirring occasionally. Reduce heat, continue to stir occasionally and simmer until milk is reduced to about 1¼–1½ cups (about 15–20 minutes). Cool to room temperature. Stir to break any large chunks.
2. In a separate bowl combine evaporated milk, thickened milk, sugar and essence. Stir to dissolve the sugar. Pour milk mixture into kulfi containers or ice cube trays (makes 2 trays). Freeze until solid. I sometimes freeze in popsicle makers for kulfi on a stick.
3. Transfer into ice cream bowls and garnish with crushed pistachios, if desire.

Makes 12 servings
Serving size: ¹/₁₂ recipe

Exchanges: 1 starch
1 milk
1 fat

Amount per serving:

Calories	185	Carbohydrate	26 g
Fat	6 g	Dietary fiber	0 g
Saturated fat	3.8 g	Protein	7 g
Cholesterol	24 g	Sodium	108 mg

Bibliography

1. *The Healthy Weigh, a practical food guide*, The American Dietetic Association,1991
2. *Maximizing the Role of Nutrition in Diabetes Management*, American Diabetes Association, 1994
3. *Exchange Lists for Meal Planning*, American Diabetes Association, American Dietetic Association, 1995.
4. Bowes and church's *Food Values of Portions Commonly Used*, 16 th edition, Jean A. T. Pennington, J. B. Lippincott Company, 1994.
5. USDA Agriculture Handbook # 8, Composition of Foods, 1989.
6. *Nutritive Value of Indian Foods*, C. Gopalan, B.V. Rama Sastri, and S.C. Balasubramanian, National Institute of Nutrition, Indian Council of Medical Research, Hyderabad, India, 1989.

Recipe index

293

Vegetables

Chicken

Fish

Meat

Yogurt, salads and chutneys

Index

Order form

Piquant publishing

P.O. Box 784
Ames, IA 50010

Phone: (515) 292-7170
Fax: (515) 292-5234

Your Order for Lite and Luscious Cuisine of India

Telephone orders: Please have your credit card ready.
Fax or mail orders: Please fill the form below.

Payment amount

Amount for _____ copies at US $19.95 per copy $ _____

Shipping and handling:

    $2.95 for first copy, $1.00 for each additional copy $ _____

    For USPS Priority Mail, add $1.00 per copy $ _____

Iowa Residents: add 6% Sales Tax $ _____

                                           Total $ _____

Method of payment

☐ Check, payable to *Piquant Publishing*

☐ Visa
☐ MasterCard   _____   _____

                                    Account Number   Exp. Date

_____   _____

        Name as it appears on the card   Signature

Your address

☐ Mr. ☐ Mrs. ☐ Ms.   Name _____

Address _____

City _____ State _____ Zip _____

Telephone: Day: _____ Evening: _____

Order form

Piquant publishing
P.O. Box 784
Ames, IA 50010

Phone: (515) 292-7170
Fax: (515) 292-5234

Your Order for Lite and Luscious Cuisine of India

Telephone orders: Please have your credit card ready.
Fax or mail orders: Please fill the form below.

Payment amount

Amount for _____ copies at US $19.95 per copy $ _____
Shipping and handling:

  $2.95 for first copy, $1.00 for each additional copy $ _____

  For USPS Priority Mail, add $1.00 per copy $ _____

Iowa Residents: add 6% Sales Tax $ _____

                                        Total $ _____

Method of payment

☐ Check, payable to *Piquant Publishing*

☐ Visa
☐ MasterCard   _____   _____
                        Account Number   Exp. Date

_____   _____
    Name as it appears on the card   Signature

Your address

☐ Mr. ☐ Mrs. ☐ Ms. Name _____

Address _____

City _____ State _____ Zip _____

Telephone: Day: _____ Evening: _____